PSL Guide to
Backpacking Photography

Ted Schiffman and
Susan Lariviere

PSL

Patrick Stephens, Cambridge

ISBN 0 85050 551 7 (HB)
ISBN 0 85059 552 5 (SB)

Acknowledgements

We would be remiss if we failed to acknowledge the role played by each of the following people in the conception, and completion of this book. Our thanks go:

IN THE BEGINNING:

To Sidney Schiffman, my father, for giving me my first Nikon camera.

To Aaron Jarit and Bob Friedman of Carol Studios, Lynbrook, New York, for helping to cultivate my early interest in photography, and for being such good friends.

To Ansel Adams for his inspiration, and guidance during his Yosemite workshop on The Making of a Photographic Book.

DURING:

To our parents for their patience and understanding.

To Roy Silverstein for his invaluable assistance in the darkroom, and in the field.

To Richie Higgins for his interest, and expertise as a model.

To all our photography friends at the New York City Sierra Club for their support.

To Ted, for believing I could write it.

To Susie, for writing it.

AND ETERNALLY:

To Teddy Roosevelt for starting the National Parks System, and to John Muir for helping us to appreciate it.

Dedication

*To our son, David, for joining our world
and sharing our joys.*

OTHER BOOKS IN THE PSL GUIDE SERIES

Contents

Double Arch, Arches National Monument, Utah. 28 mm lens.

Introduction

This is a book about backpacking and wilderness photography. It has all the basics for the avid backpacker who would like to take a camera, the avid photographer who would like to try some backpacking, or someone who is trying both for the first time. After a few outings you'll no doubt develop your own system, but in the meantime, this book can help you get started with what to pack, how to pack it, and how to get those outstanding photographs that will let you relive your wilderness experience at home. Along the way, you will probably develop an increased sensitivity to nature and a new way of perceiving and experiencing your environment that will add to your enjoyment of both backpacking and photography.

As intended here, *backpacking* should not be confused with *mountaineering*. Admittedly, the backpacking experience includes mountain-climbing expeditions, but it is by no means limited to that intense level of involvement. As long as you are carrying provisions that will allow you to be self-sufficient in the wilderness, even if they are nothing more than a snack and a few extra rolls of film, you're a backpacker. No matter how short a planned outing, you can still take advantage of the freedom and independence your self-sufficiency provides, both personally and photographically, for wilderness photography is one of the things backpackers can do best.

The connection is logical, for the wilderness abounds with photographic subjects. Backpacking merely allows you to carry the equipment you need to take advantage of that fact. Being a self-sufficient entity you are free to hike alone, reaching secluded places infrequently visited by casual strollers. You gain access to a greater variety of photographic subjects because you can travel farther than a photographer who needs to be near his tent or car. The ability to get to where the crowds are not, is invaluable in the National Parks. The quiet beauty of undisturbed areas can be a welcome change from the well-trampled environments of the more popular trails, and if you are well supplied, there's no need to leave.

This brings us to the most important benefit of backpacking: time. Good wilderness photographs don't happen all by themselves. You have to find your subject and determine both the angle and composition before you even begin to click the shutter. All this, no matter how automatic it is to you, takes time; time to explore and tune into your environment; time to experiment with your equipment; time to experiment with your ideas. Backpacking gives you the time and the freedom to stay in the wilderness for as long as you like.

At first, it seems impossible to do such completely different activities as hiking and photography. Hiking is a mobile activity, photography a stationary one. Doing one, therefore, automatically precludes doing the other, for unless you are making a movie, you can't photograph while you are walking. How do successful backpacking photographers resolve this contradiction? To be able to concentrate on both at the same time requires a special way of walking in, and relating to, the environment, the "how to" of photographic backpacking.

Before we begin, let's make one final distinction between two very similar sounding terms: *backpacking photography* and *photographic backpacking*. Backpacking photography, or wilderness photography, is the collection of images this book will hopefully help you to create, and the science of creating those images. Photographic back-

packing is the unique way a photographer hikes in, and re-
lates to, the wilderness to locate good photographic subjects and provide an atmosphere that is conducive to
creativity. In short, the secret to successful backpacking
photography is in mastering the techniques of photographic backpacking: the photographer's approach to hiking.

There's more to successful backpacking photography than just hiking with a camera. 16 mm full frame fisheye. © 1980 Roy Silverstein.

1

A Photographer's Approach to Hiking

The first step in understanding the techniques of photographic backpacking is to understand the nature of the photographic backpacking experience. Just what do backpacking photographers do? Obviously, they do some hiking, and take some photographs, though usually not at the same time. They hike, then stop to take pictures, then hike again. At least that's what the term *backpacking photography* implies; a little backpacking and a little photography. The impression that backpacking photography is a cut-and-dried alternation of disjointed activities, couldn't be further from the truth. Even though they are not going *click* all the time, successful backpacking photographers are continuously involved in the photographic process, either by consciously seeking out photographic subjects or by subconsciously attuning themselves to the environment. Backpacking photography, is a concurrent involvement in two activities which enhances the enjoyment of each.

Let's explore the dual role of the backpacking photographer. First, how does it differ from that of the backpacker in general, and what changes have to be made to incorporate photography into the backpacker's wilderness routine? The most obvious difference is in how much you will carry. Camera, film, tripod and lenses will add a substantial amount of volume and weight to your pack. If you don't want to change how much you carry, then you'll have to change what you carry. Things you used to pack will have to be left home to make room for your camera equipment. No matter how much you carry, there will be changes in how you carry it. Unlike most of the equipment backpackers stow away, photographic equipment must be packed so that it is readily accessible, reachable, and usable. Even if you don't have to stop hiking to get at your camera, you'll still have to get accustomed to occasionally removing your pack to improve your ability to photograph.

There's more to successful backpacking photography than just hiking with a camera. True backpacking provides you with the independence and equipment you need to take advantage of the countless exciting photographic subjects awaiting discovery in the wilderness. The key to finding them is not in where you go, but how you get there. Being in the right place at the right time can be important, but not nearly as important as being sensitive to what is around you.

This point is worth emphasizing, for we are often channeled in a completely opposite direction when trying to improve or expand our photographic skills. Think of the questions asked a photographer by people who admire, or want to try to duplicate, a particular image he has taken. Often the first thing they want to know is the kind of camera used. This question is invariably asked by disgruntled Instamatic users contemplating the purchase of a 35 mm camera. The answer they are looking for is not "a 35 mm camera" but a brand name, as if one type of camera can create an image that another brand cannot. The questions that follow are often: what lens was used, what f-stop and shutter speed? These questions indicate a familiarity with the captions of numerous "how to" camera magazines.

This approach, of teaching photography through a discussion of equipment, is unfortunate, for it puts the emphasis in precisely the wrong place. Having identical equipment does not guarantee identical results. You may learn from the experience of others, but you cannot duplicate that experience, especially in wilderness photography. The wilderness is not a still life. Seasons change, flora and fauna live, grow, and die. Even knowing precisely where, and at what time of the year, a photograph was taken doesn't ensure finding the same thing when you get there. A field of flowers, one year, may be a drift of snow the next. A favorite tree may have become a victim of the wind. Even if the subject is still there and is relatively unchanged, you're a different person with different perceptions and sensitivities, which will be reflected in your photography. Even the same photographer will respond in different ways at different times.

Where should the emphasis be placed when learning photography through the experience of others? Not on where to find what others have photographed, nor on the kind of equipment used. Emphasis should be placed on how to most effectively use the equipment you've got, and on how to photograph what appeals to you.

Too often people overlook the personal aspect of photography. Photography is a personal art form. The tools of our trade may be the same, but what we photograph, and how we photograph it, is very much a matter of individual choice. We each experience the wilderness in different ways, and we each photograph it differently.

As personalized as photography is, there are still some basic principles and techniques that can improve the quality of your backpacking photographs, no matter what level of involvement you choose. The answers to the two most immediate questions ("What do I pack?" and "How do I pack it?"), depend on your hiking experience, and are discussed in Chapters Two and Three. Once you have your equipment in the field, the most important question becomes, "How do I use it?".

Getting good images is really a two-part problem. First, you have to locate your subject. Then you have to determine the exposure angle, and composition. Finding the subject is not the same as finding the image. Some things you see just don't work photographically, and some things you end up photographing probably didn't catch your eye at first. How to create images on film is considered in detail in Chapter Four. Here we are discussing the issue of finding your photographic subject, turning our attention to hiking. How you hike, and relate to the wilderness, determines both the type, and quality, of photographs you take.

Your pace and stride, how you hold your head and

Tune in to the environment. Develop a comfortable pace.
28 mm lens. © 1980 Roy Silverstein.

pack, whether you sing, talk, count, or day dream, whether you walk with companions or alone is the way you hike. All of these will be affected by stopping to find photographic subjects. The way you hike determines how *tuned in* to the environment you are, how much you see, hear, and feel.

The importance of involving all your senses cannot be stressed enough. Photography is a visual medium, and we are a visual being, but the wilderness is more than visual. True, we cannot transmit the sounds and scents of the wilderness through our images, but by becoming sensitive to all that is around us, we can create a feeling on film.

This is a quality of art that is not limited to photography. A two-dimensional object, limited in area, fixed in time, inanimate, unchanging, can appear life-like, three-dimensional, transmitting emotion and sensation it is incapable of possessing. Only by developing a sensitivity to your environment, its sights, sounds, and smells, can you create a photograph which tells how it feels to be there. You cannot create a feeling photographically if you are unaware of it personally. No matter how automatic your camera is it doesn't take the pictures, you do. Only sensitive photographers create beautiful images. Insensitivity yields sterile two-dimensional snapshots. Become a part of your environment, feel it, sense it, on every level. Let your camera become an extension of your senses and you'll end up with photographs that capture the feeling of where you are.

WHAT A BACKPACKING PHOTOGRAPHER DOES

All of the pleasures and skills of photographic backpacking are based on this. They create an atmosphere that fosters sensitivity, and consequently your photographic creativity. They provide you the time you need to locate, and work with good photographic subjects. They increase your ability to perceive and respond to your environment.

Now let's carefully analyze just what a backpacking photographer does in the field:

Look for patterns and repetitions of form. They are subtle but important compositional elements. 200 mm with 2 X extender.

Locate

Find the photographic subject.

Respond

Simultaneously with finding the subject. Maybe it's actually your emotional response to the subject that made you notice it as a photographic possibility. It's often because we respond to something on an emotional level that we notice it on a physical level.

Perceive

Identify and label the response. Decide why you've noticed the subject, why it's appealing, repulsive, intriguing, or awesome. By labeling and interpreting our response, we transform an emotional involvement into an intellectual one.

Sort/Select

Decide what you want to accomplish photographically. What you want to photograph, why you want to photograph it, and the feeling the image should convey.

Manipulate Equipment

Select your lens and angle, possibly revising your earlier conclusions as you perceive your subject through the camera's eye.

Execute

The emotional and mental processes complete, *click*, and the image is yours.

Repeat

Repeat the above until all the photographic possibilities that intrigue you—different subjects, angles, lenses, and exposures—have been exhausted.

Backpacking photography requires physical, mental, and emotional involvement. The presently popular *point and shoot* school of photography, with its emphasis on speed, has reduced our concentration to only location and execution. If you are interested in creating the best images you can, you'll understand the importance of all seven steps, and consequently, the importance of time.

Time is the single most important factor in developing, and practicing, the skills of backpacking photography. It takes time to locate good photographic subjects, to develop a feeling for the environment, to decide what you want your images to convey, and to experiment with your equipment. Take the time you need while hiking in the wilderness, and you'll not only do more but enjoy more, both personally and photographically.

THE TECHNIQUES OF PHOTOGRAPHIC BACKPACKING

Walk slowly

The most important thing an experienced backpacker can do to successfully incorporate photography into his hiking experience is *slow down*. You'll see more, and get a better look at what you see. Relationships that are difficult to perceive—light and shadow, parallels, reflections and duplications of forms—will become visible, and make your images more effective. You'll see smaller things (flowers, mushrooms, toads, etc.), subjects normally camouflaged from casual viewing.

One of the nicest things about walking slowly is that it's easier to do. Since you don't have to watch your feet as much as you do when rushing, you can spend more time concentrating on where you are, and on where you are going. This, coupled with the fact that you'll be spending more time on the trail, means you'll have more of a chance to become attuned to where you are. This, in turn, will improve the quality of the images you take home.

Estimating Hiking Time

When you've slowed down, you'll undoubtedly discover that it takes longer to hike the trail than the sign at the trail head suggests. You'll be walking slower and stopping frequently, for extended periods of time. This necessitates some adjustments in how, and where, you hike.

Overestimate the amount of time you will be on the trail. A one-hour trail may take you two to three hours, or even all day, if you find something worth watching as the light changes.

Allow yourself this flexibility. Bring extra food and film, so you won't be forced to leave sooner than you want to. Try not to make arrangements to meet people at a specific time. Subconscious pressures to hurry up, and get somewhere, can impede your creativity. You may enjoy being where you are a lot more than where you planned to be.

Change the focus of your attention from where you are going to how long you will be out. Most hikers start with a destination in mind, and estimate how long it will take them to get there and back. Instead, determine how long you can stay on the trail, and then see how far you get. You may get to the end and back sooner than you think, or just 100 feet into the environment and there all day. Allow yourself to be unpredictable. Freedom and flexibility are what backpacking's all about.

Destinations

We're all a little too goal oriented. "How far did you travel?" is not as easy a question to dismiss as "How long did it take you to get there?". Even if no one is there to push us on, we can't help wondering what we'll miss by not hurrying down the trail. Few trails make loops. Most have specific destinations—a lake, a pinnacle, a spectacular waterfall—which are obviously worth hiking to, or the trail wouldn't be there. It's difficult to stay in one spot, or even walk slowly, with such an unquestionable attraction beckoning. It's difficult, but not impossible.

Observation of countless hikers racing off to the trail's end and returning with a "it's no big deal" expression on their faces will quickly convince you it's worth trying. How much did they miss along the way? In a rush to get where they're going they have had no chance to discover where they've been.

Be Comfortable

Wear clothing that is suitable for both hiking (not too tight around the knees, good walking shoes), and for photography (don't be afraid to lie down in what you're wearing to get a better shot of that mushroom). Don't carry more than is comfortable. A heavy load can affect you in two ways. First, it can tire you out, and put a damper on your ability as well as your desire to take photographs. The pack itself

Be comfortable. Wear clothing that is suitable for both hiking and photography. 50 mm lens. © 1980 Roy Silverstein.

can inhibit your freedom of mobility, an integral part of photography, and removing and replacing the pack to get a better shot or a different lens may not seem worth the effort. On the other hand, carrying a heavy pack tends to lead to a slower pace and more frequent rest stops, both of which help to increase your awareness of the environment, and therefore greater photographic involvement.

The difficulty of the terrain also affects your interest and ability to photograph, much in the same way a heavy pack does. Rough terrain slows you down and tires you quickly, but the most important way it impedes your photographic endeavors is by causing you to have to concentrate on where you are stepping. You have to think about what you are doing every foot of the way. You develop a tunnel vision, a narrowed field of concentration which tunes out the surrounding environment.

There's also a positive aspect to this seemingly anti-photographic approach. As your sensitivity to your surroundings decreases, your perceptions of the world at your feet increases. You concentrate on those stones in your path, you begin to really see them for the first time. Things usually overlooked are now subject to careful scrutiny. Is it any wonder that rough terrain has a tendency to produce abstract and macrophotographs?

There's another positive aspect to intense concentration. You develop a greater awareness of what it feels like to be in, and move in the environment. This feeling, in every muscle, and bone, can do more to develop your sensitivity to the surroundings than any casual scanning of the eyes. If you're trying to document the hike, or capture the feel of it, you'll be a much better photographer for the experience.

CAPTURING THE FEEL OF THE ENVIRONMENT

Walk Quietly

Keeping quiet decreases the birds and wildlife you frighten away, and increases your ability to hear the sounds of the wilderness. Sound is a very important per-

How do you capture on film what it feels like to be in the wilderness? 28 mm lens.

ception, and can help you locate potential photographic subjects—a bird in a nearby tree, a brook, a marmot whistling near its den.

Hiking with Companions

One of the problems with hiking with others is that talking increases the noise level and changes your concentration from photography to conversation. It's difficult to absorb signals from the wilderness while you are emitting responses to questions, or absorbing comments from a companion. Unless you are both engaged in similar photographic activities, it's hard to walk slowly and quietly to concentrate on photography. There's more pressure to "hurry up and go" and less of an incentive to "try it from one more angle." Admittedly, hiking is less lonely, and often more meaningful when shared (not to mention more fun) but companions can be a mixed blessing for a photographer.

If you do find a compatible hiking partner, you're really in for a treat. Two people can carry twice as much as one. If you are both photographers, you can carry a greater variety of equipment than if you hiked separately. With two sets of eyes, and two sets of perceptions, you'll discover more photographic subjects, and possibly greater avenues for creativity. Working together can be inspirational, as long as you maintain your individuality and don't try to copy what the other person is doing. Try something new, share each other's experiences. You should still end up with different images.

Even if your companion isn't a photographer, there are other advantages to not being alone. If you're concerned about missing something up ahead while photographing, your companions can put down their packs and walk on ahead to scout things out. Chances are they'll prefer doing that to staying put with nothing to do. You'll then have less pressure to get going, and they'll have less of a feeling that you're taking too long to get moving. It's like being in both places at the same time.

Choosing your Subject

All of the preceding techniques are designed to increase your awareness of your environment. But often, even with this newly developed sensitivity, some people still aren't successful at locating good photographic subjects. The explanation is simple.

Sometimes when you're totally immersed in an environment it's difficult to pick out what you want to photograph. Your impressions of the place are formed by the impulses bombarding your senses. Your vision is widened by sounds from behind you and afar. You don't have to turn around to see the stream you hear rushing over slippery, cool stones; nor do you have to touch it to know what it feels like. Wind rustles through the leaves in the trees overhead and the sound of it is enough to bring to mind the dappled effect of the leaves in the shadowy light. How can you capture it all on film? How can you imprison on a two-dimensional piece of paper what it feels like to be in the wilderness?

When you're there it's difficult to decide what specific photographs will adequately represent the whole. After you are home, in a different environment, it is easier to understand what pictures you should have taken. Our memories help us sort out the things that meant the most to us. When you are in the field, walking, sensing, experiencing it all, it's not as easy to pick and choose.

There are two explanations for this inability to decide on what to photograph. Being in the wilderness is either overwhelming or underwhelming. It can be overwhelming if you dwell on the limitations of your photographic equipment and the infinite expanse of wilderness you are trying to capture. Of course you'll never get the sounds on film, or the smells or feel of the wind. But how do you get that tree, the whole tree, with the woods and meadow below? You've tried a wide-angle lens, then a wider one, but the more you try to squeeze into the frame, the more distorted it all looks. You just can't seem to make it all fit, for so much is going on you can't possibly take pictures of everything. Overwhelmed by it all, you put away your camera and rationalize that pictures just aren't the same as being there.

Rather than be overwhelmed by a field of flowers, let the field itself become your subject. 28 mm lens.

When you're there, it's difficult to decide what photographic pieces will adequately represent the whole. (Joshua trees, southern California) 28 mm lens.

Also, some people can't decide what to photograph because they are "underwhelmed" by it all. Standing in the heart of the wilderness, surrounded by endless stands of trees, near rivers that twist through acre after acre of meadow, on a sand dune in a desert that stretches as far as the eye can see; they come away with a "If you've seen one, you've seen them all" attitude. Why bother to take a picture of that tree when there's one just like it over there, and another over there?

To help explain this "what's so special about it?" problem, there's an analogy in family picture taking that's worth discussing. Film and camera companies have begun campaigns to try to educate their consumers on what constitutes good family photographs. People have a tendency to take out their cameras only on special occasions—birthdays, anniversaries, vacations—and end up with pictures of stiff people in groups. Are those pictures really the most meaningful to us later on? Aren't the best pictures, the most telling pictures, the ones that show us what our lives were really like—the things we did every day. Aren't the most important things those that were an integral part of our lives, and shaped the world in which we developed and grew? The most meaningful photographs capture the essence of our lives—where we work, how we play, who we see every day—not the people and events that flit in and out of our lives, the things we inappropriately call special.

It's hard to change that attitude about photography. It seems unnatural to photograph something you're doing today if you've done it yesterday, and probably will do it again tomorrow, or the friend with whom you spend your day. But if you move, your life changes. Perhaps your children want to know what it was like when you were a child. Those are the images that will say the most.

Cactus detail photographed with 50 mm lens and bellows attachment.

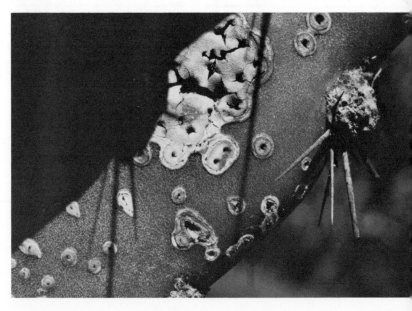

Personalize the wilderness. People can be compositional elements too. (Grand Canyon, Arizona) 200 mm lens.

The same thing happens in the wilderness. Take a picture of a waterfall, but don't forget to show us what your campsite looked like, or where you pitched your tent, and how you cooked your meals. So there's mile after mile of cactus? Take a picture of a cactus, or two or three. Someday, when you are camped among the pines, you may want to remember how the cactus looked. Once you try to photograph them, you'll see they really aren't all alike. "If you've seen one, you've seen them all" is the attitude of someone who really doesn't see.

Another complicating factor has to do with what scientists call *sensory adaptation*. When you first arrive in the wilderness, your senses are most acutely aware of the differences, be they the sounds of the night or the colors of the day. The visual, as well as aural, impact of any place is most striking when you are new to the environment. The longer you stay, the less aware you become of the sights, and sounds, around you. Crickets, June bugs, and peepers that seem so deafening quickly blend into the background. The more time you spend in one spot, the more difficulty you will have in deciding, "what's so special about it?". Trust your first impressions and take photographs right from the start.

But there is also something to be said for taking photographs after you've been located in one spot. First impressions are important, but so are lasting impressions, the ones that develop slowly and stay with us for a long time. They may give you a completely different photographic approach from the one you used initially. You've had more of a chance to become familiar with indigenous flora and fauna, the typical climate, the typical terrain. You've had a chance to get to know the environment. All this may help you decide what to photograph. When the overwhelming main attraction has had a chance to blend into the background, you'll have more of a chance to concentrate on those little things you might have missed.

The essence of good backpacking photography is to let there be a free flow and exchange between the wilderness and you. Perceive and respond, personally, and photographically, on a moment by moment basis. As the wilderness changes, so let your photography. Day to day, hour to hour, blade of grass to blade of grass, there will be different things to see and feel. All of it is exciting to discover. All of it is potentially an exciting photograph. As you relax and become one with the wilderness, comfortable with it and in it, your photography will reflect more and more of the creativity within you.

*When deciding what to take, don't forget the little ones.
With a Gerry Pack, hiking can be an experience for the entire family. (Near Matterhorn, Zermatt, Switzerland) 55 mm
macro lens.*

2

How to Decide
What Equipment to Pack

Your ability to take photographs depends a great deal on
how you feel, and your comfort will be determined by several factors. Where you are hiking (Is the terrain easy or
difficult? Is there an altitude problem?), how much you are
carrying (Is it too heavy a load for your physical condi-
tioning and the terrain?), the climate (Is it very cold or very
hot, will you have to deal with hyperthermia, heat exhaustion, glaring sun, sudden downpours, or snow?).

The above will determine how much equipment,
food, and clothing you can carry comfortably. Obviously,
the less you carry, the less self-sufficient you can be, the
less time you can spend on the trail, and the closer you
have to stay to base camp. But remember, the important
thing is not how many miles you hiked or how many hours
you were out, but rather how fruitful and enjoyable the excursion was. The quality of your photographic subject
isn't determined by the quantity of time it took you to walk
to it. Some of the best photographic subjects can be found
closer than you think.

FACTORS

You do, however, want to be efficient, to carry as little as
possible so that your creativity won't be hampered by discomfort. But not so little that insufficient equipment limits
your photographic possibilities. Remember, that deciding

what to pack involves more than just cameras, lenses, and film. There are other pieces of camera equipment to consider (tripod, filters, strobe, etc.), but more importantly, there are food, clothing, and in some cases, shelter. Though every backpacking experience is different, and no matter how experienced you are, there's always something you've brought that could have been left home, and something at home you should have brought. Here are some basic suggestions about what to carry:

Determine your level of involvement

Will it be an overnight hike, a day trip, or a few hours? Do you have to carry a tent, cooking gear, sleeping bag, etc.? Essential camping gear should be packed first.

Will photography be the primary activity?

How important is having a variety of camera equipment available? Will you take only what you can get into the space remaining in your pack, or is there a minimum of camera gear you must take, even if it means carrying a larger pack? Is camera gear all you really need, or is it only something you'd like to take if you have enough room? The professional photographer, or serious hiker, who wants to document each phase of a backpacking experience will require a great deal more photographic equipment than the casual National Park stroller, who wants to have a camera handy just in case he sees something he likes.

The intent of your photography, as well as your hiking, determines your gear: the things you must have, to the things you'd like to have, to the things you can probably do without. The most important realization of all is that you must make a selection. You can't possibly carry everything you might use. The primary determinant of what to pack is how much you can carry.

Know your weight limit

No matter how short or long your hike, or how casual or serious your photography, there are some things you must have with you, and others you'd just like to have. Be realistic about how much you can carry. Now is not the time to decide to build yourself up by carrying a little more weight than you are used to. If you've never backpacked before, don't decide you can carry a load because it felt comfortable when you were wearing it for five minutes in your living room. A pack feels very different when you've worn it for a while, when you're traversing up a mountainside or stepping over rocky paths. Underestimate what you can carry comfortably. Be sure you can remove and replace the pack by yourself. The whole purpose of a pack is to allow you to be self-sufficient in the wilderness, to enable you to carry the equipment you need to photograph where you are and what you are doing. If you allow the pack to become heavy and cumbersome you are defeating the whole purpose. You'll have little incentive to take photographs if you're not enjoying your hike, and there's no way to enjoy it if you are uncomfortable.

Know your equipment

It's important to be both comfortable in, and with your equipment. You should be familiar with all its intricacies and able to handle them with great facility. The only way your camera can become an extension of your senses, and

It's important to be comfortable both in, and with, your equipment. 50 mm lens. © 1980 Roy Silverstein.

help you respond to your environment, is if your movements are second nature. You should be able to focus, change apertures, lenses, and film, quickly and automatically, as though your subconscious were doing the work while your conscious mind searches for potential images.

Only this way will you be able to channel your energy into the creative aspects of photography. Equipment you have difficulty using, that malfunctions, jams, or otherwise acts strangely, is equipment you are not going to want, or be able to use. Unused equipment, on a backpacking trip, wastes space and adds weight that you would be more comfortable hiking without. To prevent this from happening, here are a few recommendations:

First, don't borrow things. So your cousin has a brand-new super-expensive camera that's loaded with features he'll let you use on your trip? Avoid the temptation. Take only things you know how to use well.

Second, don't take new things you are not accustomed to. Give a new piece of equipment (pack, camera, tripod, strobe, zoom lens, etc.) a dry run before you take it on a backpacking trip. Learn its idiosyncrasies before you leave, and if convenient, test it to see if it is functioning properly.

Third, refresh your memory by trying out your old equipment. It won't take long for your facility with it to return, but it's easier and more convenient to do at home.

Fourth, have your equipment cleaned, checked and repaired sufficiently ahead of the trip to get it back from the repair shop in time. Don't forget to check your batteries! If there's a piece of equipment you're not sure of, and there's no time to get it checked out, leave it home. No sense having it break down in the field or, even worse, having it malfunction without your knowing it and ruin your images.

You and your camera equipment should be like old friends, comfortable and natural together, working and moving harmoniously, almost as one. There are times you'd like to experiment with something new—a new film, a new lens—but don't overwhelm yourself with a pack full of new equipment. You won't have the time, nor the energy and incentive, to wade through it all in the field. You want to enjoy the wilderness, not take an extensive camera course while hiking.

Know the terrain

Find out the difficulty of your hike. In frequently hiked areas this is easy to do. Some trailheads and information brochures specify easy/difficult, or give an estimated hiking time for the trail. If the amount of time allotted for the trail seems excessive for its distance, it's because the trail is steep, or composed of a material that's hard to walk on. If you can't find this information directly, consult a topographical map. Look at the change in elevation, as well as the elevation of the base area. Even if you are not climbing any higher, just walking at 10,000 feet may be difficult.

Knowing the terrain can help you in two ways. It will help you decide what to carry (special foot gear, for example), and how much to carry. The harder the terrain, the lighter your pack should be.

Know the photographic possibilities

Will you be hiking through a thick rain forest, or glaciers? Will there be mountaintops with sweeping panoramas? Eagles nesting in distant trees? Unobstructed views of breathtaking sunsets? Knowing the answers to questions like these helps you decide several things.

What kind of film you should use

Will you need a fast film, or will there be sufficient light for one with a slower ASA rating? Lighting conditions do fluctuate, and you should carry different kinds of film, but it's good to know in advance which kind you are most likely to use, so that you can have your camera loaded and ready with extra film nearby.

Which lens should be most accessible

No matter where you are hiking, you'll have opportunities to use a macro lens. You should also know if you'll have numerous wide-angle scenics, or once-in-a-lifetime telephoto wildlife photographic possibilities. Knowing the photographic possibilities helps you decide which lens should be on the camera, which should be handy, and which can be packed away.

Which accessories you will be likely to use

Will you use your tripod for almost every shot? If so, better not pack it away. Will you want to use a strobe for fill-in flash, or to freeze the action? If so, better not leave it at home. Investigating ahead of time as to what to expect can eliminate much of the guesswork in packing.

Know the climate

Hot and cold climates have different effects on our ability to hike and take photographs. Extremes of either can make any activity difficult, but being prepared can alleviate most of the discomfort. Weather can vary but, in a given place at a given time usually only within certain limits. Plan ahead to protect your body.

Feet

A good pair of hiking boots can handle a variety of terrains, and weather conditions. You might consider supple-

Gaiters, essential for hiking, snow shoeing or cross-country skiing, should also be worn in tall brush or wet grass. Camera case manufactured by Safari. (Note: camera strap should always be placed around your neck.)

menting their protective properties with a pair of gaiters, nylon spat-like shields that attach to your boots and cover to your knees. Gaiters are essential for hiking in snow, or walking through brush. You might need to use a silicone spray on your boots for added waterproofing. Take extra socks in case your feet get wet, or perspire excessively.

Hands

The main problem you can expect with your hands is keeping them from getting numb in the extreme cold. Normal amounts of stiffness due to loss of circulation in cold weather becomes a real obstacle when trying to take photographs. Metal, especially on your tripod, is difficult to work with in subfreezing temperatures, unless you wear gloves. Gloves provide added comfort, but you sacrifice a degree of dexterity. Mittens provide maximum warmth, but eliminate dexterity altogether. There are also other problems associated with working in extreme cold which have nothing to do with personal discomfort. These are discussed later in the book.

Eyes

Some people who work in sunny places regularly don't wear sunglasses because they find them to be distracting, uncomfortable, or even a hindrance. Other people complain they get a headache if they don't wear them. Whichever category you fall into, you'll find you're able to function photographically, only if you keep your sunglasses on all the time or off all the time. Putting them on to look around, and taking them off to look through your viewfinder, becomes a nuisance very quickly. Besides being one more thing to worry about, sunglasses make it difficult for your eyes to adjust to harsh changes in light over and over again. Perhaps that's why you never see a professional tennis player or golfer wearing sunglasses. They want to see it all, just the way it is, in one consistent lighting situation. As a serious photographer, so should you.

There are situations where you will find you have to protect your eyes in a special way. Strong winds that can dry your eyes, wind-blown sand that can scratch your corneas, and snow-reflected sunlight that can damage your retina. All these situations call for wrap-around sunglasses. (Some people call them mountain-climbing glasses because they are sold in mountaineering stores for people who hike on glaciers.) They are far from cosmetic, but when they are needed, they are the best kind of protection.

Camera gear.

Your photographic equipment has to be packed differently to protect it in different kinds of weather conditions: rain, sun, heat, dust, snow, extreme cold. The how-to of packing will be discussed in Chapter Three, but it is mentioned here as a reminder that you are not the only one affected by the weather.

DEVELOP A SYSTEM BASED ON EXPERIENCE

Everyone's photography is different. The best way to determine what to bring is to go out on several excursions and see what is used most often, what is used occasionally, and what is not used at all. Sooner than you think, you will develop a system that works for you, what to pack, how to pack it, and what to use in each situation. It is this experience, more than anything else, that can tell you what you should have with you on your next trip.

Of course you can't expect to develop that system if you have difficulty remembering exactly what you used in the field last time. When you are out there you think, "How could I ever forget?", but once home you quickly do. In the beginning, or if your trips are infrequent, take a notebook with you and write in it when "I wish I had" or "Why did I bother bringing this?" flashes through your mind. If you have any special terrain, weather conditions, or problems you've solved, write them down. The more detailed your notes on any given trip, the easier it will be to pack for the next one.

Companions

Will you be hiking together, step-by-step? Are they photographers? Maybe you can share equipment, or maybe someone can carry something for you. Naturally, you'll be much better off if you carry all your equipment yourself, but you may be flexible in this area. If you're afraid you won't be able to carry all your camping gear maybe someone can carry it for you.

ESSENTIAL EQUIPMENT

No matter what your specific situation, all backpacking photography needs the following essentials.

Cameras

A second camera, though an additional weight, allows you to use two different films simultaneously (Kodachrome 25 and High Speed Ektachrome (ASA 400), for example) and/or to have two different lenses mounted, and instantaneously available.

Film

Lighting in the wilderness is extremely variable, so you'll need both slow and fast film. When packing, remember there's no such thing as excessive amounts of film. "Excessive" is saved for gear that becomes useless, dead weight in your pack. You can take photographs in spite of some forgotten piece of equipment, but when you run out of film you're out of everything.

Lenses

A variety of lenses allows you to achieve a variety of results, but it's far from necessary (or practical) to own every lens available. Even if you could afford it, you certainly couldn't pack, carry, and use them all. Here, more than anywhere else, it pays to be efficient. Which lenses should you take? A good rule to follow is to double your focal lengths. Here's a very complete example:

- 16 mm full-frame fisheye (an extreme wide-angle that gives you a rectangular image, not the round image of the standard fisheye)
- 28 mm wide-angle
- 55 mm micro (a standard and close-up lens)
- 105 mm or 135 mm (a short telephoto)

Changing lenses changes your photographic statement. (Grand Canyon of the Yellowstone) 85 mm and 200 mm.

200 mm *or* 300 mm (a longer telephoto)
500 mm
1000 mm

This way you have a wide range of possibilities. You wouldn't carry both a 105 mm and a 135 mm lens, because they are so close in focal length. Similarly with a 24 mm and a 28 mm wide-angle lens, the difference in image isn't worth the added weight.

Zoom lenses are another way to maximize your flexibility, while minimizing both the number of lenses you carry and the number of times you change lenses. A 50–300 mm zoom lens will do the work of three of the lenses in the previous example.

Using zoom lenses is another way to maximize your flex-ibility. 50-300 mm zoom lens shot at minimum and maximum focal lengths.

There are advantages to zoom lenses, but there are also advantages to fixed-focal-length lenses. The standard properties of a 55 mm macro lens may be replaced by a 50-300 mm zoom, but its macrophotographic capabilities can't be. Though the range of the zoom lens clearly covers portrait focal lengths, an 85 mm may open to f/1.8 while a zoom lens may only open to f/4.5. If you want a fast lens, take your 85 mm. Another extremely workable combination of lenses is:

16 mm
28 mm
55 mm macro
85 mm
50-300 mm zoom
500 mm
1000 mm

Long telephoto lenses, such as the 500 mm and 1000 mm lenses mentioned above, may at first seem impractical for backpacking, and indeed standard long lenses are. However, there are catadioptric, or mirror, lenses in these focal lengths which are perfect for the backpacking photographer. They are shorter, and lighter than standard tele-

Sunlight sparkling on ice-covered boughs. 500 mm catadioptric (mirror) lens.

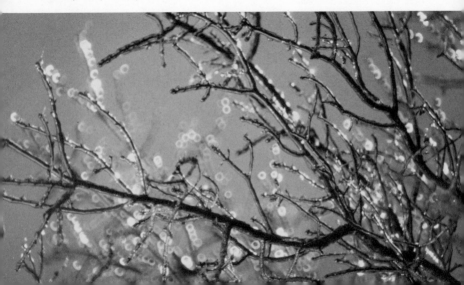

photos. The light entering these lenses is bounced around by mirrors before it hits the film. Their size and weight make them easy to carry and use. Besides being lighter, the fact that they are shorter than standard telephotos makes them less front-heavy, and less cumbersome to hand-hold.

What you gain in weight, you lose in speed. Most mirror lenses have fixed *f*-stops (for example, *f*/8 on the 500 mm and *f*/11 on the 1000 mm lenses mentioned above), which give you a very short depth of field. Exposure corrections can only be made by changing the shutter speed, so in low-light situations you are almost always forced to use a tripod.

Another difference between standard lenses and mirror lenses is that with mirror lenses areas not in focus have donut shapes. This special effect can lend a unique soft quality to backgrounds, which frames your subject. This is especially noticeable when photographing sunlight reflecting off water, dew drops on blades of grass, or dappled sunlight in trees.

The choice of which lenses to bring therefore depends on where you are going, how much you are carrying, and, what you already own. Your hiking companions might have some lenses you can borrow, but it's not a good idea to count on it.

Tripod

A good tripod for backpacking photography is small, light, sturdy, and versatile. It should be small and light enough to be carried in your pack, sturdy and versatile enough to provide you the support and creative capabilities you want in the field. The heavier the tripod is, the harder it is to move once set, but the light ones suitable for backpacking are surprisingly stable. When selecting a tripod look for the following properties:

1. Can you extend the legs and raise the shaft to look through the viewfinder without stooping or bending over? Is the full-upright position of the tripod sturdy enough to support the weight of your camera, motor drive and telephoto lens? Does it feel top-heavy, and easy to knock over, in this position?

A good tripod for a backpacking photographer is small, light, sturdy and versatile, such as this Gitzo Total Luxe Performance, The Gitzo Weekend Compact Performance and the Slik 500 or 800. © 1980 Roy Silverstein.

2. Do the adjustments tighten sufficiently to support your camera, motor drive, and telephoto lens in any position without slipping? This is something you should allow sufficient time to check. Slippage happens slowly, isn't easy to detect and has two very negative results. First, it forces you to constantly reframe your image. Secondly, it forces you to steady the lens while taking the photograph, creating the possibility of camera shake, something the tripod was supposed to eliminate.

3. The center shaft should be reversible, so that your camera can be mounted between the legs of the tripod, in an upside-down position, for macro, and close-to-ground work.

4. The legs should be flexible enough to allow you to get your camera close to the ground in either the right-side-up or upside-down position.

With all of the above properties, your tripod will be one of the most versatile and essential tools for your backpacking photography. Whatever the frequency of use, it still will be an indispensable piece of equipment.

Accessories

The following photographic accessories are worth considering:

Filters: A *polarizing filter* reduces glare, and saturates colors by absorbing the light reflected off surfaces, and can be rotated to change the amount of absorption. It deepens blue skies, and allows you to see through the surface of water, much in the way polarized sunglasses do.

Colored filters: (Red, green, orange, yellow, blue, etc.) are for special effects, their most dramatic use being with black-and-white film. When used with color film, "what you see is what you get."

Strobe: For dark forest floors, fill-in flash on backlit or partially shaded subjects, and to freeze fast subjects, such as hummingbirds.

Reflector: Any small bright material (aluminum foil) can be used for fill-in or supplemental lighting much in the way a strobe would, though not nearly as effectively.

Meter: Hand-held, to read the exposure directly off your subject when you feel the averaging meter in your camera may not be giving an accurate reading. Used for high-contrast situations, strong backlighting, subjects on snow fields, and reflective backgrounds, such as water.

Cable release: To eliminate camera shake caused by hand depression of the shutter button.

Maintenance equipment: Lens tissue, brush, pressurized air, plastic bags, and a small screwdriver for tightening screws on camera and lenses.

Extras

Batteries for your light meter and motor drive.

Packs and Bags

What you use to carry your equipment depends a great deal on how much you have to carry. There is quite a range of options:

Camera bags: Over the shoulder leather or canvas bags with compartments and pockets for your camera, lenses, and accessories. You can get a few "munchies" in

Over-the-shoulder camera bags, such as the Eric System Bag, can rest on the small of your back while you're hiking and be swivelled around for convenience while photographing. © 1980 Roy Silverstein.

there as well, but these bags are generally best only for short day hikes.

Knapsacks: Small backpacks designed for day hikes. These can be used for photographic purposes, but if you need something inside they must be removed from your back.

Backpacks: Medium to huge, framed and un-framed, are suited best for overnight and long-term hiking. They hold the most but are hardest to take photographs while wearing. They must be removed for maximum maneuverability.

CAMPING ESSENTIALS:

Hat, rain gear, knife, first-aid cream, snake-bite kit, band-ages, tissues, toilet paper, aspirin, foot pads, extra socks, clothing and food.

The choices of what to pack for photographic back-packing excursions are as varied as the types of back-packers and photographers. Take what you feel you need and can carry comfortably but don't forget to make a note of what was a good or bad choice. You'll be amazed at how quickly you'll learn what's right for you. If you are unsure of your selection, don't start your backpacking experi-ences off with an ambitious overnight trip. A serious mis-take in what you brought will be something you'll have to live with for what seems a long, long time. Start off with a short hike, an easy walk from your base camp or car. This way you can go back, and start all over again if you want. But, chances are, even the first time out your choices will be right.

A frequently-used long lens might be more conveniently carried on your hip than in your backpack.
© 1980 Roy Silverstein.

3

How to Pack and Carry Your Equipment

Photographic equipment must be protected from dust, heat, strong sun, high humidity, water spray and vibrations. It must also be accessible enough for use without unnecessary inconvenience.

Accessibility is very important. Obviously, you can't carry all your lenses on your camera. Some of them have to be packed away, but a lens that is easy to get to is one you will use often. A lens that forces you to unpack and repack each time, will probably not be used at all. This severely limits your photographic possibilities, and the lense become an unnecessary weight to carry, occupying space in your pack that could have been used for something else.

The same thing is true of photographic accessories, such as a tripod and filters. Things you use often should be readily accessible; things you use infrequently, less so. Once in the field, you may find your priorities changed since you prepared for your trip. A little reshuffling of your pack may be in order. A few minutes spent reorganizing your pack is better than constantly fishing through things you don't need.

By far, the most important element in successful packing, however, is knowing where everything is. This involves two aspects.

First, have a set place for each piece of equipment, and use these places consistently. Don't change where you put things; it will make it easier to find what you want in a

Accessible equipment is the key to creativity. You'll use what you can most easily reach.
© 1980 Roy Silverstein.

hurry, and also help you remember what to pack. If you see a section of the camera bag is empty, you'll know what has been forgotten.

Secondly, pack things so they can't move around in your bag. If you put your 28mm lens on the left side when you packed it, it should be on the left side when you go to use it. Keeping the lens secure, helps you find it quickly and helps protect pieces of equipment from damage. If you are using a knapsack, or some other pack which doesn't have built-in compartments, you can devise your own dividers and protectors for the equipment.

For some people, packing for a trip is difficult, but, in reality, the hardest part is deciding what to pack. Take everything you intend to pack and spread it out on the floor. This will help you decide how big a backpack, or camera bag, you will need. The ideal thing is to take the smallest bag you can. You want to be as comfortable as possible, and a smaller pack will be easier to work with. As a photographer, you will be using, not just transporting, the contents; items at the bottom of a small pack are far more accessible than those in a large pack.

The next step is deciding what goes where. Check your field notes from previous hikes and see if your recommendations apply to this trip as well. If you are backpacking in a new terrain, or doing a different kind of hiking, they may not, but some things remain the same no matter where you go. If this is a first experience make a list of what you are packing, and how you are packing it, and supplement the list with a photograph of your gear. If the first attempt at packing turns out to be a winner, you'll be thankful for this detailed record on your next trip.

The following are some examples of how you can pack your equipment. What's best for you is something only you can decide as your backpacking experiences change.

An over-the-shoulder canvas bag (such as the Eric System Bag), with pouches and compartments for lenses and accessories, is extremely versatile for the backpacking photographer. It can be used for one-hour jaunts, or full-day hikes, alone or in conjunction with an additional small backpack. The accompanying chart shows one possible se-

Sometimes two bags are better than one. The backpack is stationary and can accommodate your non-photographic gear. The lower, over-the-shoulder camera bag, can hold your camera equipment and be swivelled around to the side for greater accessibility. © 1980 Roy Silverstein.

With careful planning, your equipment can be packed to meet all of your basic photographic demands. See the facing page for a detailed breakdown of how this one has been arranged.

lection of photographic and camping items and how to pack them. As the photo illustrates, there is plenty of room for food, but water should be carried in a hip canteen. The camera and lens are shown here packed. When they are removed the bag has even more room for additional items.

POSSIBLE SHOULDER BAG ARRANGEMENT

Compartment	Items Packed (bottom to top)
left pouch	toilet paper (cardboard removed), foot pads, snakebite kit, first-aid kit, Swiss Army Knife, suntan lotion, wrap-around sunglasses (plastic), Chapstick, Listerine (for bug bites), 5 rolls of film
left front compartment	4 lenses with packing foam (16 mm, 28 mm, 55 mm macro, 105 mm), camera to be carried
middle front compartment	500 mm mirror lens, bags of silica gel
right front compartment	extra camera body with meter, 200 mm lens wrapped in extra socks
right pouch	small belt-clip pouch with small bellows, lens-cleaning tissue, Static Master brush, air-brush bulb (brush removed), extra batteries, rubber eye cup, strobe, lens-cleaning solution, portable screwdriver set, polarizer, cable release, 5 rolls of film
rear compartment	fold-up rain suit, Gitzo tripod with head removed, motor drive, hat
zippered compartment	tin-foil reflector, note pad, pen, maps (not shown)

The following product photos are from various manufacturers who make equipment suitable for backpacking photography. In most cases each manufacturer produces several models of these items. The variety of equipment is expanding rapidly and the few examples presented here only give you a small sampling of what's available.

The Domke Bag is a shoulder bag with optional backpack strap. Photo courtesy of DOMKE BAGS.

Ultimate Experience Photographer's Backpack

Mojo Harness Strap.

The Cannondale Removeable Bike Bags convert to shoulder bags.

Richmond/Merritt Harness Camera Case.

The Tamrac Holster Pack also converts to a chest or shoulder pack.

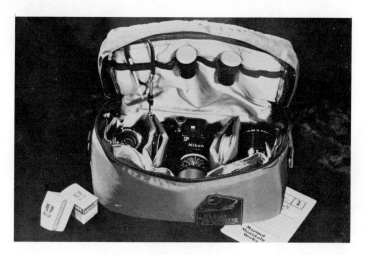

The Mojo Fanny Pack is a compact and convenient way to
carry photographic equipment.

Sunset through milkweeds. 55 mm macro (close-up) lens.

4

How to
Use Equipment
in the Field

The most important factor for success in the field is preparation before leaving home. This is the foundation which makes the experience that follows possible.

First, and foremost, you must be physically ready for your excursion.

Have you have chosen the right equipment, and carefully packed it so that it is both protected and accessible?

Do you know where each piece of equipment is packed, so that you can find it quickly?

Are you familiar with, and have confidence in, your equipment? Is everything functioning well, properly maintained, and easy to use?

Are you prepared for changes in weather while you are hiking? Dark clouds rapidly approaching on the horizon may threaten rain, but don't be afraid of getting wet, for they could be just one more dramatic element in your photographic composition.

If something goes unphotographed, it shouldn't be because you did not realize that it was unusual. Read up on where you will be hiking, in order to know what to look for and to be able to identify it. Familiarize yourself with indigenous flora and fauna, and what to expect during the various seasons.

If you are properly prepared you can relax and enjoy your hike. There will be no pressures to interfere with your ability to concentrate on where you are and what you are doing, and no pressures to inhibit your creativity. Physical preparations affect your mental stage, and go hand-in-hand with psychological preparations. The most important psychological preparation is recognizing the complexity of the photographic operations ahead. It's not just point and shoot out there. That's what this chapter is all about.

As mentioned in Chapter One, locating your photographic subject is really a four-part operation; locate, respond, perceive, and select. Though the wilderness abounds with an infinite variety of potential photographic subjects, you make a choice based upon your own personal relationship with the wilderness and with photography. You not only decide *what* to photograph, you also decide *how* to photograph it, for selecting your subject is not the same as selecting your image. Recognizing that there are many ways to interpret one subject, manipulate yourself and your equipment (changing the angle, composition, the focus of attention within the frame) in search of the image you want. The more carefully you investigate your photographic possibilities, the more pleased you will be with your results. Just as there are processes to help you select your image, there are also processes to help fine tune that image. These can make the difference between a good photograph and an outstanding one.

COMPOSITION AND LENS SELECTION

Composing your image involves several things. Deciding what to photograph, *the subject*; where it will be situated within the frame, *the placement*; and what kind of emphasis will be placed on it within the frame, *the statement*. One of the restrictions of photographing the wilderness, and its most fundamental challenge, is that you have to work with what's there. Unlike the illustrator, who can put the perfect bird on the perfect branch, you don't always find what you want where you want it. Perhaps it's this difficulty in obtaining outstanding photographs that makes them, to some people, more exciting than good illustrations.

Assuming that you are not going to disturb the natural environment, how do you transcend limitations of subject and placement to make the photographic statement you want? The techniques are many, but begin with an understanding of the true order of operations in the field.

One common misconception is that you first find your subject, then decide how you want to photograph it, and that determines which lens you use and your shooting position. This isn't altogether true.

A common exercise in beginning photography classes is to have the students shoot a couple of rolls of film using only one predetermined lens. An immediate reaction is "I can't take the pictures I want," "I need my wide-angle lens," or "I need my telephoto lens." We often see a subject and then translate it into the lens that will include or eliminate what we want in the viewfinder. But, instead of changing lenses, the problem can often be circumvented by moving closer to, or farther away, from the subject.

Using only one lens breaks you away from shooting only preconceived images. It teaches you to see as the camera sees, to look at the world through your viewfinder, letting it suggest what to photograph. By doing this you learn how the lens determines the statement you can make. When you're satisfied that you've captured the desired image with the lens on your camera, try another lens. A new perspective may surprise you, be exciting and successful.

Lenses serve two purposes: they allow you to reproduce preconceived images exactly the way you want, and they are tools for experimentation. It's not until you experiment that you will discover your true creative potential. Through experimentation you will discover the vast range of capabilities of each and all of your lenses, and the kinds of things you alone can do with them. It is experimentation, more than anything else, that fosters the development of personal style.

Changing lenses changes composition in several ways. It determines how much information is included within the frame, for a wide-angle lens includes more than a telephoto lens. Lenses determine the size of the subject, how close it feels to the viewer. A 500 mm shot of a distant bear yields a photo with a larger subject than a 50 mm shot. There are also less obvious effects of lenses. Extreme wide-angles warp vertical lines near the edges of the frame, while telephoto lenses usually compress distance, making distant objects appear closer to foreground objects. Also, the range of f-stops on your lens determines both the lighting conditions under which you can use that lens, and the corresponding depth of field. Lens selection is one factor which determines the photographic statement you can make by determining what is included, what is in focus, and the strength or subtlety attached to the main subject.

SHUTTER SPEEDS AND F-STOPS

There are two ways to change the amount of light entering the camera and striking the film. One way is to change the length of time the shutter stays open. (A shutter speed of 1/60 of a second keeps the shutter open longer than one of 1/500 of a second.) The other way is to change the size of the

Shutter speeds can be selected to freeze water or to accentuate its motion by letting it blur. These photographs were shot at a shutter speed of 1/1000 sec. and 1/2 sec. 28 mm lens.

lens opening. An aperture of *f*/16 is smaller than one of *f*/1.4 and admits less light. Your exposure meter tells you the combination of shutter speed and *f*-stop that will give proper exposure. It will probably also show you that several combinations of shutter speed and aperture work (for example, *f*/8 at 1/500, or *f*/11 at 1/250, or *f*/16 at 1/125). Which one you use is one of the most important factors involved in fine tuning your image.

In some situations, the combination of shutter speed, and *f*-stop does not matter. But more often than not, you will find yourself either in a shutter-speed, or an aperture, priority situation. A shutter-speed priority situation is one in which the shutter speed you use, because of the nature of the photograph, is crucial. This could be either very fast or very slow. In these cases the *f*-stop you use will be determined by the shutter speed necessary. There are three major areas in which shutter speed is crucial: water motion (covered in Chapter Five), camera shake, and fast-moving wildlife.

Camera Shake

The best way to minimize or eliminate camera shake is to use a tripod, but if you don't have one, or can't place it correctly, you can still hand-hold your camera. The trick is to not use any shutter speed slower than the reciprocal of the focal length of your lens, or, if possible, even half of that. For example, if you are using a 105 mm lens, you should use only shutter speeds faster than 1/105 or 1/125 sec. (1/125, 1/250, 1/500 sec., etc.). If you are handholding a 200 mm lens, shoot at 1/200 or 1/250, sec. or even faster (1/250, 1/500, 1/1000 sec. etc.). This is especially important when hand-holding telephoto lenses, which have a tendency to accentuate the effects of camera shake. Apply this rule, and you will realize why the effects of camera shake on wide-angle lenses are so negligible. You rarely have occasion to use a 28 mm lens at speeds slower than 1/28 of a second.

For macrophotography the rule is even more severe. The reciprocal of your focal length, even half of that, isn't fast enough. A 55 mm micro lens, for example, should be used with shutter speeds of 1/125, 1/250, or 1/500 sec. to ensure maximum clarity.

Wildlife

Even if your camera is securely attached to a tripod, there are times when you must use fast shutter speeds to freeze the action of a moving subject. If you are attempting available-light photography of fast-moving birds, and don't have the stop-action potential of a strobe, you will still be able to capture a lot by using your fastest shutter speeds. Those cardinals at your bird feeder, the woodpecker in the tree, the chipmunks in your campground, may be still for a moment and darting the next. Head movements are generally erratic, but swift, so at slow shutter speeds sharp body poses can be spoiled by blurry heads. If animal behavior (as opposed to animal portraiture), interests you, then you'll have to use your camera to freeze the action. The wildlife won't do it for you.

In all of the preceeding situations the shutter speed you select is of primary importance, but there are also instances in which the *f*-stop you select is more important than the shutter speeds. These aperture-priority stituations are not as easy for the beginning photographer to comprehend, and take a little more explanation.

DEPTH OF FIELD

The *f*-stop does more than just determine the size of the iris opening of the lens. It also determines the depth of field—the size of the area which will be in focus—and has a tremendous impact on your photographic statement. The largest number (for example *f*/32), corresponds to the smallest iris opening and yields the largest depth of field. The smallest number (for example *f*/1.4) corresponds to the largest opening and yields the shortest depth of field. Nature scenes with several elements or subjects (for example a waterfall with surrounding foliage and flowers) look especially striking when all elements are in sharp focus. Single subject-photographs (for example a flower) are most effective when your in-focus subject is framed by the soft out-of-focus blur a short depth of field creates. Depth of field can be used to create very different feelings within your photographs.

One of the reasons depth of field has such a strong effect on the viewer has to do with the nature of the photographic image. As a two-dimensional representation of a three-dimensional subject, a photograph is greatly affected by anything that deals with the lost third dimension. One of the marvels of the medium is that it can create visually what is not there physically: a sense of depth and distance as objects move into, and leap out of, a flat surface. Streams flow from the far distance (the top of the photograph), to the very spot where we stand (the bottom of the photograph). Grass and flowers stretch up from the

Nature scenes with several compositional elements are especially striking when all those elements are in sharp focus. Maximum depth of field resulted from using smallest aperture, f/22. (Merced River near Yosemite, California) Normal lens.

earth (the bottom of the photograph), and then arch forward as if to touch us.

By manipulating depth of field you can enhance the three-dimensional quality of your images, reinforce the sense of movement, and create framing effects that focus attention on the central subject. While most cameras allow you to select your *f*-stop, evn if you have to switch to manual override, practically none of the lenses actually change the size of the iris opening until the shutter button is depressed. Consequently, the depth of field in the viewfinder is that which corresponds to the lowest *f*-stop on the lens. Changing your *f*-stop doesn't change the depth of field you see in the viewfinder, but does change the one you'll see in your photograph. The extremes of depth of field, corresponding to smallest and largest *f*-stops, are easy for us to visualize. Understanding the effects of those in between, and selecting the one that works best, is more difficult. Fortunately some cameras have a depth-of-field preview button, which makes selecting your *f*-stop simpler because it makes it visual.

Single subject photographs are effective when the in-focus subject is set against an out-of-focus background. Short depth of field resulted from using a large aperture, f/5.6. 55 mm macro lens.

Depth-of-field preview button

By depressing the depth-of-field preview button you can look through the viewfinder to determine two very important refinements for your image: the depth of field, and its placement.

There's no general rule as to what depth of field corresponds to which f-stop. It's a function of several variables: the lens, the f-stop, and the distance from the camera to the central point of focus. The most important thing to know is that the higher the f-stop number the deeper the field of focus. When using a 50 mm lens set at f/4, and focusing on a flower ten feet in front of you, you are apt to find that everything from nine to twelve feet away will be in focus. However if you were to use the same lens set at f/16, everything from six and a half to twenty-seven feet would be in focus. The best way to decide which f-stop you want is to press the depth-of-field preview button as you change f-stops, and see which treatment creates the desired image. Most lenses also indicate the depth of field of different f-stops on the lens barrel.

In addition to deciding how much of your photograph should be sharp, and how much should be blurry, you should also decide where the blurry areas will be. Suppose, as in the previous example, that six feet in front of you (four feet in front of the flower), lay a dew-covered bed of moss. Even with your camera set for the maximum depth of field, f/16, the moss may be out of the area of focus, and look disturbingly blurry in the foreground. Suppose you are content with your choice of lens, where you are standing, your angle, f-stop and shutter speed combination, and don't want to change any of them. How can you get both the moss and flower within your field of focus? By moving the point of focus. Instead of focusing on the flower, focus a little in front of it (say eight feet in front of you). This way depth of field will be between 5½ and 15 feet. Your main subject (in this case the flower), needn't be placed in the exact center of your field of focus. Let your depth-of-field preview button tell you where to place the sharp area of your image. Moving the f-stop ring will make the depth of field deeper or shallower. Moving the focusing ring will move the area in focus closer or farther away.

When a photograph comes out looking as though the depth of field was too short it means some things came out blurry that should have been in focus. This situation can be avoided by careful placement of the camera, and its angle. For *f*-stops with short depth of field, keep the areas you want in focus parallel to the plane of your film. This is especially true for macrophotography (which is notorious for short depth of field problems). When photographing a mushroom, for example, you might want to get both the stem and the rim of the cap in focus. These two areas will not be in the same plane if you place your camera in a standard head-on position. The part of the rim closest to you will be blurry when the stem is sharp, or the stem will be blurry when the front of the cap is sharp. Changing the angle of your camera, tilting it up and lowering it closer to the ground, puts the stem and the cap in the same plane of focus. Use your depth-of-field preview button to see where to place your camera to give you, and your images, a new perspective on a familiar subject.

Compositional balance

The benefit of the depth-of-field preview button comes hand-in-hand with one of its major difficulties. By closing the iris of the lens down to your selected *f*-stop (allowing you to see the corresponding depth of field) you admit less light into your camera. The picture you see gets noticeably darker as you stop down to smaller and smaller apertures. Sometimes it gets to the point where it is hard to see anything in the viewfinder, let alone the depth of field. But, this situation can help you with another aspect of fine tuning your composition: balancing light and dark areas.

Balancing objects within the frame is the key to good composition. Where they are placed affects how the eye moves across the image. Much of the impact of your image depends on where the eye is drawn, whether attention rests on one subject, or moves back and forth among several. Eye movement is also affected by the location of light areas within your photograph. With the naked eye, the effect of bright areas on a potential photograph is hard to determine. We normally perceive the continuity of light, and concentrate on the forms of our subjects not their brightness. But film sees only light. A good photograph is one in which areas of light and dark are as carefully placed as the subjects themselves. Your depth-of-field preview button can help you see, and place, areas of light and dark.

The darkening of the viewfinder after pressing the depth-of-field preview button, has the effect of eliminating the differences between objects with mid-degrees of brightness. Dark areas are still dark and light areas are still light, but the middle ground, the medium tones, blend together. By using the depth-of-field preview button you will be able to see the dominant bright areas that might have gone unnoticed—hot spots where the sun bounces off a rock in a stream; the chrome on your friend's tripod; or the petals of a nearby flower. By seeing where they are, you can decide whether to place them. You can choose a new position or lens, wait for the sun to shift, or decide you wish to shoot it that way.

The contrasting light and dark areas created by dappled sunlight, when carefully placed, can enhance your composition. 85 mm lens.

Photographs taken in dappled sunlight are notorious for hot spots and high contrast. But, if used correctly, dappled sunlight can create very strong images. If ignored and left to chance, it can create photographs that are very hard to print. High-contrast lighting makes it impossible to maintain the detail in both light and dark areas. Though your eyes can perceive the details in extremes of light, film will end up with silhouetted dark areas, and washed-out light ones. Using your depth-of-field preview button can help you decide what you want, and where you want it within the frame. It's one more tool which can help you see as the camera sees, to know in advance what your photograph will look and feel like.

PRECOMPOSING AND CROPPING

One of the advantages of printing your own images, or having custom prints made, is that you get a second chance at deciding on your composition. If your original image contains a distraction you didn't notice when you took the photograph, such as a car parked between the trees on the right, you can crop it out when you make a print. Anything you can crop out of your image in a darkroom you can crop out in the field by placing the camera differently, or by changing lenses. There are several reasons why you should crop your images when you make them.

First, a cropped duplicate transparency, or copy negative, will never have the quality of an original. Secondly, the less handling and manipulating the original gets, the longer it will last. Thirdly, enlargements made from parts of a frame show grain to a greater degree than those made from the whole frame. Your film is small, and should be used efficiently. Most importantly, it's better photography to crop your images in the field. It forces you to apply all the elements of good composition, training you to eliminate objects you don't want, and to be more careful about how you arrange them.

One of the mixed blessings about wilderness photography is that you are working in a constantly changing environment. Clouds roll in and out of your viewfinder, changing shape as they go. The wind rustles the leaves in the forest's canopy, changing the amount of light hitting the forest floor. The sun's movement across the sky may not be noticeable to us, but constantly rearranges the high-lighted leaves and foliage.

If your composition is perfect, take the photograph. In a few minutes, or seconds, what you see in your view-finder may be very different. If what you see isn't quite right, you probably won't have long to wait to get a very different light. It's more exciting, than frustrating, to work in an environment like this, for it makes the feeling of hav-ing captured a moment in time all that more powerful.

YOUR TRIPOD

The tripod can extend photographic capabilities more than any other single piece of equipment. It allows you to take photographs at extremely low shutter speeds for time exposures, and when using the small apertures necessary for maximum depth of field. It allows you to take multiple-frame panoramas, and with a self-timer, allows you to take pictures of yourself.

A tripod helps prevent fatigue caused by hand-holding long lenses over an extended period of time. When taking several photographs of the same subject, such as a bird roosting in a distant tree, let your tripod hold the cam-era and lens, for it keeps your viewfinder at eye level far longer, and far more comfortably.

By freeing the hands, a tripod makes fine tuning your image easier. Hand-holding a camera creates a tend-ency to concentrate on framing the subject, on holding the camera still enough to prevent the composition from changing at the borders of the photograph. With the tripod holding the camera the framing is secure, so you can turn your attention to the finer elements of your composition: cropping, depth of field, and exact point of focus. It be-comes easier to focus, and to check the depth of field, and its placement, as well as manipulate the aperture/shutter speed combinations.

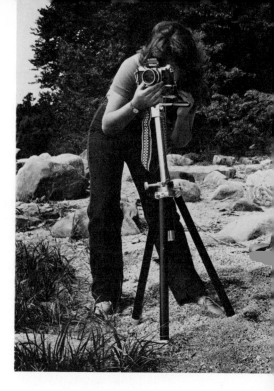

By freeing both of your hands, a tripod makes fine tuning your composition easier. © 1980 Roy Silverstein.

Whenever time and terrain allow, use your tripod for razor-sharp clarity, maxiumum depth of field, and the freedom to concentrate on the finer elements of composition.

Using the Tripod

The most important thing to know about your tripod is how to set it up quickly and quietly. A tripod that is difficult to set up, manipulate, and compose with, is one you won't use very often. If setting up is work, you'll have less incentive to take advantage of the unique photographs a tripod helps create. Practice with it at home, and refresh your memory before each excursion.

In the field, don't set up your tripod until you know exactly where you want it. Determine the camera position, composition, lens, angle, horizontal or vertical format, then place the tripod and mount your camera.

Fine tuning your composition will be easier with your camera mounted on the tripod, but the broader precomposing processes are easier when hand-holding your camera. Move around with your camera until you find the perfect spot for it. Then set up your tripod. The camera should determine where the tripod will be, not the other way around.

Learn to place your tripod quickly and quietly. This may take some practice, for the legs may telescope out with a sliding noise, or the central column might drop with a bang. Make sure the camera is securely attached, and the legs and other adjustments are locked in place. Remember to check for slippage, for a slow tipping downward of the lens can change your carefully determined composition. For best camera stability, and accessibility, place the tripod so your feet are between two of its legs, with the third leg pointing away from you.

Fold up your camera strap, so it does not dangle in your way, become tangled in your clothing, or accidentally hook onto your arm. Put the strap over your neck when working near water or a precipice.

When taking photographs in unusual places you will begin to discover the finer features of your tripod. There are rubber tips on the legs for slippery areas, and points for anchoring into the ground. The legs can be adjusted to different heights for terrain that isn't as uniform as your living room floor. Some tripods can be lowered practically to the ground or the central column inverted to shoot down on things between the legs. How you set it up depends on what you want to photograph, and where you are standing. With most tripods you should be able to do just about anything you'd like.

If you find yourself in the rare situation where you cannot get your tripod into proper position, try the alternatives: stand somewhere else, use a different lens, or try a different angle. Your new perspective may turn out to be as good, or even better, than the one you originally wanted.

Carrying the Tripod

There are three different ways you can pack and carry your tripod. You can tie it to your pack, or camera bag, so it is accessible but out of your way. This is the best way for

Where the footing is secure and your tripod is needed frequently, it can be carried as a unit with your camera. © *1980 Roy Silverstein.*

outings where you will be using the tripod only from time to time. You can also leave your camera mounted to the tripod, and carry the two of them as a unit on your shoulder. This is the best way for outings where you will be using the tripod for just about every photograph, for it saves time unpacking, and setting up. (On difficult trails, or trails with unsafe footing, you will want both of your hands free and therefore shouldn't carry your camera and tripod this way.)

For trails with a variety of photographic opportunities, keep one camera with a long lens mounted on your tripod, and another camera with a wide-angle, or zoom, lens around your neck. This way you have both the security of a tripod and the freedom of a hand-held camera, without having to disconnect or unpack anything.

Finally, you can leave your tripod at home, and rely on makeshift "tripods" in the field. This is the best way for outings when you are not apt to use the tripod at all, or for times when packing and carrying your tripod is difficult. Though they are less reliable, and less predictable, than a tripod, you'll be surprised at how many stabilizers you can find in the field.

Make-shift Tripods

Your pack or camera case. There are lots of special devices you can use to adapt your equipment for stabilizing purposes including a clamp with tripod head that you can secure to the frame of your backpack. These specialized pieces of equipment are discussed further in Chapter Three.

The ground. Most suitable for forest-floor macrophotography, but remember to keep your camera and lens clean, dry, and free from obstructions. Place the camera on a small piece of plastic, if you have one, before resting it on the ground. When resting your camera on a flat surface, you will have to use something (your camera strap will do), to keep the lens propped up.

A zippered "bean" bag. You can make your own portable "bean bag" out of an old pants' leg. Sew it up on one side, and put a zipper on the other. Instead of filling it with beans, fill it in the field with dirt and leaves. When you are finished using it, you can dump out its contents and pack the empty bag away.

Stumps, rocks, logs, and branches. Be sure to prop your camera securely, to keep it and the lens clean, and do not disturb the natural environment.

When using something other than a tripod to support your camera, make sure it is securely held in place.

Logs and rocks are just two stabilizers, or artificial supports,
you can find in the field. © 1980 Roy Silverstein.

The weight of the lens may cause the camera to tilt downward. Even the slight movement of the mirror as it snaps
up, and then back into place may cause a precariously situated camera to vibrate. A cable release can be helpful, for
once the camera is positioned you want to disturb it as
little as possible. A cable release allows you to take a photograph without touching the camera, thereby eliminating
the possibility of accidentally jarring it and changing your
composition.

Another way is to hand hold your camera, and let
something support you. A tree, a rock, a fence, a sign can
be used to steady yourself and your arms while you take
the photograph. Sometimes, all you need is something to
rest the barrel of your long lens on, or a stick to use as a
monopod. When your camera feels lighter, you are able to
hold it steadier. Finding something to support just a part of
the camera's weight may be all you need.

SHOOTING POSITIONS

The problems with hand-holding a camera and long lens
are very similar to those of holding a target rifle. The
longer you hold a camera or rifle, the heavier and heavier it

When hand-holding your camera, leaning against something, such as a tree, can increase your stability. Open camera case by Safari.

feels. The tendency to shake increases with time, and your ability to concentrate on anything other than keeping steady decreases. That taking photographs is also called shooting is not coincidental, for the techniques used to steady a rifle can just as effectively be used to steady a camera.

There are four major aspects: *position, breathing, shutter control,* and *follow-through.* The goal is to help you obtain maximum stability without artificial support. In each of the following four positions you will see how to use your bones, not your muscles, to support the weight of your camera and lens. Muscles eventually fatigue, causing you to quiver and shake, but when properly balanced, your bones can support you indefinitely.

Standing is the most frequently used position for photography. Unfortunately, this is also the most difficult one to stay stable in when using a long lens. For that reason, the following discussion starts with the simplest position, prone, and works up to standing.

Prone

While lying on your stomach, raise your right leg slightly (left leg straight, right knee bent). This gets your weight off

Prone. 50-300 mm zoom lens. © *1980 Susan Lariviere.*

your stomach and onto your pelvis, relieving the pressure on your viscera. Support the camera with two hands and your face. Keep your arms close to one another, and your elbows in tight, close to your chest. Put more weight on your left arm, so that your right hand can press the shutter button without disturbing your balance or position. Ideally, your whole body should be at a slight angle to your subject.

Sitting

Cross-legged. Support the camera with your two hands and face, while resting your elbows on the inside of your knees, and your knees on the sides of your boots. Boots get your knees higher than sneakers while pads between your boots and knees get them higher still.

Open-legged (knees bent). Rest your arms against the sides of your legs, with your knees in the crooks of your elbows. The open-legged sitting position gives you more height than the cross-legged position, but is less stable.

Sitting position #1. 50-300 mm zoom lens. © *1980 Susan Lariviere.*

Sitting position #2. 50-300 mm zoom lens. © *1980 Susan Lariviere.*

Kneeling

Put your right knee on the ground, your left knee at a 90-degree angle to the ground, and sit back on your right heel. If this is uncomfortable, you may want to put something (such as a small roll or stuff-bag) under your right foot. Support your camera entirely with your left hand, and rest your left elbow on the flat spot of your left knee. Your left forearm and leg should be in a line perpendicular to the ground. You should not need to use any muscles in your back leg or foot to keep you in position. Your right hand should be completely free.

Kneeling. 50-300 mm zoom lens. © *1980 Susan Lariviere.*

Standing

Stand with your feet spread the same width as your shoulders. Put your feet at the same comfortable angle they naturally assume when you are walking. (An easy way to determine this angle is to walk a few steps, without watching your feet, stop, and then look down.) Support the camera with both hands while resting both elbows on your chest. For better support arch your back slightly, so the center of gravity of your camera is over your legs. Again, your body should be at a slight angle to your subject.

Standing. 1000 mm catadioptric (mirror lens). © *1980 Susan Lariviere.*

Breathing

Long-focal-length lenses magnify movements, so much so that even your heartbeat and breathing will affect your stability. Breathing is easier to control than heartbeat, and can be stopped altogether for the few seconds needed to take a photograph. Exhale, and hold the exhale position. It's more relaxed than trying to take a deep breath and hold the inhale position. You should be able to hold your breath for 30 seconds without feeling uncomfortable. You should be calmest somewhere between ten and twenty seconds into the interval, and that's when you should take the photograph. Any sooner than ten seconds, your body probably hasn't settled down enough. Past 20 seconds, you begin to feel the urge to breathe. If you wait until the moment is just right, you'll have one more tool to help reduce camera motion, no matter what the position used to take the photograph.

Shutter control

Hold your camera securely, but not so tight you are squeezing it (if you are, it won't be long before your hand starts quivering). You should have a firm, comfortable hold so the only thing that has to move is your shutter finger. This finger, moving ever so slightly down and up again, fires the shutter. The rest of your hand shouldn't move. It's also important to know just how much pressure is needed to click the shutter. How far down do you press the button before the shutter is tripped? These are small distances, and miniscule differences in pressure, but an important part of learning how to use your equipment. To minimize camera movement, you have to minimize hand movement. That means moving your shutter finger only as much as is needed.

Another aspect of shutter control is speed. When looking through the viewfinder at wildlife or nature scenes, you are usually waiting for something special to capture (such as a wave crashing against a rocky coastline). The procedures involved often make you wonder how it is possible to react in time. Our eyes transmit to our brains what we see, and then our brains tell our finger to fire the shutter. Knowing where the button will click, and begin just short of that point, you can speed up the process. It's like thinking with your shutter finger.

Follow-through

Follow-through is another technique to reduce camera motion. It means holding your position for a split second after the picture is taken to guarantee having held the position while the picture was being taken. If you do it correctly, you will feel as if you are holding longer than really necessary, but there is good reason why you should.

Long before you make any conscious movements your body makes unconscious movements, in anticipation of those to follow. As you press the shutter button you may already be thinking about standing up, or walking somewhere else for your next shot. These thoughts, coupled with a mind that has prematurely registered an "O.K. I'm finished," may be enough to get the body ready for its next move. A quiver here, a tremor there, a relaxing of your grip on the camera, may be slight movements, but enough to blur your image. Take your shot, and then freeze for a moment. If it's something you're glad you shot you might even enjoy seeing it in the viewfinder a little longer.

YOUR MOTOR DRIVE

The most obvious attraction of a motor drive is that it can greatly increase the number of photographs taken in a given amount of time. If you are photographing an action (such as geese taking flight from a lake, wildlife behavior, or a wading bird fishing), this increases your chances of getting what you want on film. This is the most obvious advantage of using a motor drive, but it is not the only one. Below is a list of some of the pros and cons of using a motor drive.

Pro. It increases the number of photographs you can take in any given amount of time (frames-per-second). Good for action series and fast-moving wildlife.

Con. It uses up your film a lot faster.

The sound of a motordrive often elicits inquisitive stares from your wildlife subjects. (Golden eagle). 1000 mm lens.

Pro. It allows you to concentrate on your composition, for you don't have to move the camera away from your eye to advance the film.

Con. It's heavy to hold, to pack, and to carry.

Pro. It gives your camera a big, easy-to-grip handle which makes hand-holding long lenses easier. In a pinch, you can even grip your camera in one hand.

Con. It's noisy, and can startle the wildlife you want to photograph. (If you think this will be a problem, and it usually is with birds, disconnect your motor drive, and take photographs manually while approaching your subject.)

Pro. Its noise can cause wildlife subjects to perk up and look attentive. When you have all the behavioral shots you want, reconnect your motor drive, and take some bright, inquisitive, startled portraits. If your subject, such as an elk, doesn't sprint away, he'll probably pick his head up and look directly at the source of the noise. (You needn't sound like a machine gun, one click is usually sufficient.) If your subject does flee, you're ready to record his leaps and bounds.

Pro. It loads film faster (and with an auto rewind, unloads faster), which can save time.

Con. Using the auto rewind places a tremendous drain on the batteries, and can create static electricity as the film whirls across the pressure plate. (Among other things, static electricity helps dust collect in your camera, causing scratches on your film.)

In short, along with the advantages of a motor drive come the responsibilities. It's one more piece of equipment to carry and maintain, but may be worth the effort if you get one good photograph you would have missed.

FIELD MAINTENANCE

One of the fringe benefits of becoming a backpacking photographer is that you quickly develop a respect for your equipment, and the value of maintaining it properly. Out in the wilderness you do not have access to extra equipment, or a camera-repair shop. All you can use is what you have with you, so it better be functioning properly. How you care for your equipment in the field determines how well it performs.

Proper maintenance begins with preventive maintenance. Keep your camera and lenses secure while you hike. Don't let them bump into each other, or into anything else (such as branches and rocks). Even if your equipment is immediately damaged from being jarred, the vibrations it experiences during an extended hike, or ride in a car or plane, will be sufficient to loosen screws and attachments. It's a good idea to carry a small screwdriver set, and from time to time tighten whatever needs tightening. It also pays to have a little technical knowledge of your equipment. Read your manual, and familiarize yourself with the information. Since it's small, you may even take it with you into the field.

Once in the field, it's important to keep things clean. You will constantly be stirring up dust, leaves, pollen, and sand as you hike. You will probably always have a thin coating of dust on your lens and camera body, which is why lens tissue, or some other dust remover, should be handy. You should check and clean your lens frequently. It won't matter how carefully you compose, and focus, your photograph if you take it through a dirty lens.

As bad as dust can be on the outside of your lens, it's even worse inside your camera. The film pressure plate,

High-altitude backpacking is difficult enough without the additional complications of photography, but is full of once-in-a-lifetime photographic opportunities. (Kibo peak, summit, Mt. Kilimanjaro, Africa, elevation 19,340 feet)

A telephoto lens can yield intimate close-ups of subjects far too dangerous to approach. (American Bison, Yellowstone National Park) 500 mm lens.

While you're concentrating on what to photograph, don't forget to watch where you are going. (Rattlesnake) 55 macro lens.

inside the camera, is one of the most important places to keep clean, but unfortunately it is one of the last areas people check. Specks of dust on the pressure plate turn into lines of scratches on your film. Clean the pressure plate each time you reload, using an air brush, Static Master brush, or a small can of pressurized air. (When using pressurized air remember to hold the can upright.) Also, make sure the roll of film you are loading is clean. If you accidentally drop it you might consider throwing it away, for some dirt may have entered the canister through the film slit. If so, you shouldn't use it. Also check to see if small pieces of film have broken off during loading or rewinding. (This is most likely to happen in extremely cold weather, when film gets brittle, but is possible anytime.)

Parents and young osprey at nest (Southern Florida). 500 mm lens.

Mushroom photographs needn't all be macro close-ups. Their surrounding habitats can also be captured with a normal lens. 55 mm macro used as normal lens.

When putting your camera down, place it on a clean surface that is able to support it. Your camera case, or backpack, are the best things for this purpose. If you absolutely have to put your camera on the ground, make sure to clean it carefully when you pick it up.

Also be careful to keep your camera and film out of direct sunlight. The damage sunlight can cause your film is due more to the impact of direct rays than to the heat. In the deserts of the Southwest, where the daytime temperatures can reach 125 degrees in the summer, film stored away from the sun's rays, and hot enclosures will show no trace of heat damage. Even in sub-zero temperatures, film left standing in sunlight streaming through the back window of a car, will be ruined beyond any possible use.

While using your camera you may not be able to shield it from the sun, but if you set it down, set it down in the shade. If you are not removing your camera from around your neck, turn your back to the sun, so that your body shades your camera. If your camera is mounted on your tripod, and positioned in a sunny spot for any extended period of time, use a white hat, spare shirt, or cloth to shade your camera when not in use. It's easier to remember to take care of film when it's sunny and hot, but you should also do so when it's sunny and cold.

Your tripod requires maintenance too. It's a major investment, an important accessory, and most importantly, a heavy item to carry. If it becomes unserviceable while in the field, every ounce it weighs will feel like a pound. Keep its legs clean, dry, and free of dirt and mud. Clean them before closing them up. The slightest grit can damage the telescoping mechanism, or prevent the legs from opening at all. This cleaning must be done after each use, and should be as automatic as folding the tripod up again.

When using your tripod at the beach, remember you don't have to be in the water for the legs to get wet. There's ocean spray, high humidity, and natural condensation to contend with. The same is true for tropical rain forests, and other high humidity areas. Automatically wipe those legs clean before you close them, no matter where you are.

Silhouetting is one example of dramatic lighting. Needle centered for exposure. 55 mm macro lens.

Vary your treatment of the familiar. Raindrops on the back of a tiger lily. 55 mm macro lens.

At the beach, rinse the legs with fresh water before you wipe them dry. This will eliminate your having left a salty residue on the tripod. In time, the salt will pit the aluminum, making sliding the legs in and out practically impossible.

Nighttime requires special maintenance procedures, too. As you repack for the next day, and remove exposed rolls to replace them with fresh film, remember that dew can be a problem. Pack your equipment in a large plastic bag overnight, to keep condensation from collecting on the cold metal surfaces. Then get a good night's sleep, so that you can get a fresh, early start in the morning. You are the most important piece of equipment you have. Take care of your camera, lenses, and film, but don't forget to care for yourself.

5

Head for the Water

The most obvious reason why a photographer should head for the water is that wildlife can be found there in abundance. One need not be in search of only wildlife to find a trip to the local water supply photographically rewarding.

By a stream, one can find lush plants, flowers, mushrooms, moss, and a natural contrast between the serenity of the forest and the rush of cascading water. At the ocean there are tide pools, sand formations, and the awesome power of the waves crashing against the shore. The reflections in lakes act as mirrors for sunsets and other subjects. Waterfalls, large and small, emote a feeling of power. With or without wildlife, water is where the photographic action is.

An important thing to remember about water is that you shouldn't limit yourself to only summer photographs. When it's hot, it's natural to want to go to the beach, or hike in the cool shade by a mountain stream. But every season the water has something to offer the photographer.

In winter there are frozen cascades, and rocks encrusted with an opalescent, clear glaze. The ice preserves the leaves as though in amber, on the rocks where they have fallen or been carried by the stream. Though the surface may be frozen and snow-covered, the water beneath still flows, creating caves and ice formations. The sound of the stream is muffled, but clearly beckons through the stillness of the winter forest, no longer competing with the rustling of leaves overhead. The canopy is gone, and though the days are shorter and the sun hangs lower in the sky, the stream is finally open to its brightest light. Traces of wildlife are far more visible. Deer leave paths in the snow, marking favorite trails and favorite watering spots. If you know where to look, and are willing to wait, you will find some of this wildlife to photograph.

Then comes spring—melting snow, unfolding ferns, the forest's first flowers. The songs of migratory birds echo above the roar of the swollen, rushing stream. Splashes of color appear everywhere, white snow, brown bark, yellow and red flowers. The light-green color of brand new leaves dots the naked branches of the deciduous trees, or projects from the older, dark-green leaves of the evergreens. The sun is high in the sky, and the day long, as in fall, but the canopy above is just beginning to bloom. The forest bathes in the newness of the sunshine. The warming earth is moist and rich, full of the promise of things to come. The stream is most accessible now, for the deep snow has melted, and thick weeds and undergrowth have not yet choked the forest floor. Young birds, animals, and hikers alike, celebrate the rebirth of the forest. The changes are subtle, but constant. To the unprepared, this transition, from the subtle newness of spring to the full-bodied lushness of summer, comes all too quickly.

Some people feel the forest is synonymous with summer, for that is when it reaches its maximum potential; its densest growth, lushest vegetation, maximum wildlife population, thickest canopy, and its longest, sunniest days. There's no doubt that a stream in the forest is a lovely place on a hot summer day. Just the sound of the rushing water has a cooling, soothing effect, making it a great place to be, and a great place to work.

The most photographically exciting time to be by a stream is in the fall. The crisp autumn air is exhilarating, while the shortening days yield a sense of expectation. As the weeds die, the forest floor becomes more visible and accessible. The trees will soon be bare, but not before they put on a display of colors unlike any other season. Fortunately for the photographer, this colorful spectacle isn't limited to the treetops. Leaves carpet the ground and dance in the streams, floating and twirling as the swift current carries them away. Some become marooned on moss covered rocks, others stack up in neat little piles like cards that have been filed away. The water does more than just collect the falling leaves. Like the colors of pebbles in a stream or shells in the ocean, the colors of leaves in a stream are darker, richer, and more saturated than those of leaves drying on the ground. With the surrounding moss, rocks, and bark, the leaves become the main attraction in a world of maximum color contrast.

Wildlife activity changes, too. Squirrels scamper about, feverishly making preparations for the coming winter. Birds are migrating, changing the sounds and character of the woods. One of the biggest advantages of autumn is the decline in population of the stream photographer's nemesis, the mosquito. As they decrease, your ability to concentrate, and be creative, will increase. Autumn provides a kaleidoscope of photographic subjects to challenge your abilities.

Just as the forest changes from season to season, so does the shoreline. You might have to train your eye to perceive these changes, but it will be well worth it, for you don't have to wait long to see them take place.

From hour to hour, as the tide rolls in and out again, the world at the water's edge is transformed. The best place to witness this metamorphosis is a rocky coastline; such as the Point Lobos State Reserve in California, or Acadia National Park in Maine. You'll find blow holes, caves, and tide pools teeming with life, attractions that appear and disappear with the ever-changing water level. At low tide the rocks are a wonderful place to explore for, you can get close to, and photograph, things that were totally submerged only hours before. Look for starfish, anemonies, crabs, snails, and interesting arrangements of barnacles and lichen. Sandy beaches have their attractions as well: shells, sandpipers, footprints at the water's edge. The best way to photograph the coastline is to spend an entire day watching it transform from sunrise to sunset.

There are many similarities between the watery worlds of an ocean and a stream, but there is also one major difference worth pointing out. When you spend a day by a stream it is very easy to lose track of time. The soothing sound of the water has a calming effect, enhancing the feeling that this is a good place to get away from it all. Moving shadows may be all there is to remind you that time is passing.

The sounds and rhythms of the ocean are soothing too, but one is constantly conscious of time. How soon will that wave crash against the rocks? How long till the next one rolls in? Will it reach further up the beach than the one that came before? Will it cover more of the rocks than the one that is to follow? Time is measured by recurring episodes of unpredictable duration and intensity, and by the intervals between them. Time is measured by the waves, spray, the surging swell of the surf, and the tides. More than anywhere else, the seashore is the place that tells the photographer "If you see it now, take it," for later it will be gone.

Late afternoon sun illuminates high objects while leaving close-to-ground objects in shadow. The mirror-like properties of a lake can accentuate that contrast. (Mt. Shuksan, Washington) 28 mm lens.

At different times of the day the same spot can yield a very different photographic statement.

Besides the wealth of photographic subjects, there is a psychological reason why you should head for the water. The soothing sound of a babbling brook, or the rhythmic pounding of the surf, nullifies audible distractions, and creates within you relaxing, harmonious feelings that aid your creativity.

PROBLEMS TO BE FACED

A wet environment can affect both you and your equipment.

Tricky Footing

Wet, moss-covered rocks are extremely slippery. When maneuvering among them, make sure both your hands are free to help you move around, or to steady yourself. Keep your equipment secure (camera strapped to your chest), so that it won't bang against the rocks. When positioning your tripod among rocks, make sure it has secure footing. When attaching your camera to your tripod, keep the strap around your neck.

Keeping Equipment Dry

The spray of a waterfall, or the pounding surf, can harm your equipment. It doesn't matter if you are dealing with large droplets of water, or a fine mist. Keep your equipment in plastic bags, and frequently wipe your lens clean

The winter stream's water is both frozen and flowing. Use slow shutter speeds (½ sec.) to blur its motion and maximize depth of field. 28 mm lens.

Leaf stem projecting from a stream. Moderate shutter speed (1/60 sec.) created motion in the changing water reflections. Faster speeds would have frozen the water. Slower speeds would have blurred it. 55 mm macro lens.

and dry. Store exposed film in canisters, for this will protect it from the spray and, if dropped in the water, will keep it afloat.

Even without spray, the high humidity at the ocean, or in a rainforest, presents problems of condensation on the cool metal surfaces of your equipment. At the ocean, the salt in the air makes matters even worse for it can pit the aluminum on your lenses and tripod, and leave a film on glass surfaces of your lenses. When wiping your equipment clean, use a soft, absorbent cloth. Salt will dry into an abrasive, and scratch the glass on your lens if not removed carefully. Remember to clean the aluminum on your equipment. It doesn't take long for you to hear scratching, scraping noises as salt and sand collects in the aluminum barrels of your lenses, and the legs of your tripod.

Malfunctions

Longer periods of time (such as camping at the beach over-night) can cause malfunctions in your equipment, short-circuiting, and corroded batteries. To help prevent this problem keep your equipment in plastic bags, and be pre-pared with extra batteries and a spare light meter.

Mobility

When moving among rocks in the ocean, be aware of changing wave, and tide, situations. Though the tide slowly and constantly moves in or out, an occasional wave can crash to shore much higher than those before. If you put your camera case on a rock, make sure it is in a place

Wave breaking over a jetty. A shutter speed of ⅛ sec. was sufficient to blur the fast moving wave. 55 mm macro lens.

Sunlight can add dramatic contrast to your composition. Though the sounds of the waterfall cannot be photographed, they can create an atmosphere conducive to creativity. 28 mm lens.

where it won't get wet, and that it is close enough for you to grab quickly if necessary. As the tide rolls in, remember it may cover low rocks between you and shore before it covers the one you are on. It's very easy to become so engrossed in what you are doing that you lose sight of what is going on around you. Becoming stranded on a high rock way off shore is not as unlikely as it sounds.

If you don't compensate for the reflective qualities of water (by opening up one or two stops), your subjects will be silhouetted—which may be exactly what you want. 200 mm lens.

A different angle will decrease the effect of those reflections, enabling you to get proper exposures. 500 mm mirror lens.

Tricky Exposures

Water has superior reflective qualities, creating bright areas and hot spots that make metering difficult. The problem is intensified by water that is flowing, surging, and splashing, changing the number and location of hot spots. There are some things you can do to guarantee photographic success: bracket your exposures (open up one or two stops), work in your own shadow, or wait until the sun goes behind a cloud.

Water Motion Effects

Two completely different effects can be used when photographing water: freezing the action, or accentuating its motion with a blur. Freezing water will make a stream look peaceful and calm, while blurring makes it appear forceful and determined. The ocean is a good place to experiment with both effects. There waves crash against the shore, send spray into the air, then surge back to sea. Freezing water requires very fast shutter speeds, no slower than 1/500 sec. (1/1000 or 1/2000 sec. for maximum effect). To accentuate motion, use slower speeds (between ¼ sec. and 1 second). The specific speed is determined by the speed of the current, and how much of a blur you want to create.

A wet environment has its problems, but it is one of the most rewarding places to work. Take all your lenses, film, and creative ideas, for there's an excitement, a dynamism, and an unlimited supply of subjects waiting to be captured.

Some images capture fleeting moments. Ten minutes after this photograph was taken, the rising sun melted the frost on this web. 55 mm macro lens.

6

Macroscapes

This chapter discusses the exciting world of macro-photography. Even while hiking, we rarely spend time exploring the world at our feet, or concentrate on details in nature, such as bits of bark and crevices in rocks. To do so adds a whole new dimension to the wilderness experience, both personally and photographically. The only way to discover the myriad macroscapes around us is to slow down, stand in one spot, and carefully look all around, examining and becoming sensitive to the details of our environment.

When looking for macrophotographic subjects, don't limit your possibilities by assuming that "macro" implies "small." Macro lenses allow you to get close enough to small things to make them fill the frame, but small things (such as flowers, mushrooms, and bumblebees) aren't the only things you can photograph with a macro lens. Macro-photography is close-up photography, and you can get close to big things, too. Naturally, when you do get close to a large subject you end up being able to photograph only a very small part of it. Which part should you photograph, and how? This leads us to the most overlooked, but exciting, application of macrophotography—abstractions in nature.

ABSTRACT

The variety of images you can create with macro-photography offer a rare opportunity for truly personal expression. You have more flexibility than with large sub-

This flower detail is an example of the free-form abstractions possible when you get close to nature. 55 mm macro lens.

jects which, because of their size, limit the ways you can capture them completely on film. It is only when you begin to concentrate on details, or abstractions, that you will find true photographic freedom. With macrophotography, you can select, interpret, abstract, and transform in your own unique way. Get close to a tree, and examine its bark, contours, and colors. The trunk of a tree really isn't all one color. Are there woodpecker holes, burls, or sap oozing from its crevices? Get close to the ground, and look carefully at the moss, or sand, or blades of grass. The Lilliputian world at your feet has a lot to offer.

One of the excitements of macrophotography is the thrill of discovery, the personal sense of "I found it." No matter how traveled the trail, you may have been the first to stop and stare at that mushroom or piece of bark. After you go, making sure to leave things as you found them, chances are no one else will see, and photograph, your subject. The image will be yours alone. In Chapter One it

Petrified sand formation provides an interesting abstract subject for close-up photography. (Pt. Lobos, California) 50 mm w/bellows.

says, ". . . what we photograph and how we photograph it, is very much a matter of choice." That statement is never truer than in the world of macrophotography.

SENSE OF SCALE

One of the "rules" of photography found in books for beginners is that you should have a person in your picture, or some other easily recognizable object, to lend a sense of scale. Size is one of the criteria people use to interpret what they see. Since they frequently question identity and dimension when viewing abstract photographs, a sense of scale is important to macrophotography. Yet, how do you include that easily recognizable object when you are only photographing part of it? Even if you are not taking abstract macrophotographs, the idea of making large images of small subjects is automatically contradictory to maintaining a sense of size.

How do you get around this, when the very nature of abstractions eliminates scale? Recognize that this is not a problem, but a new avenue for interpretive freedom. If you don't know the size of an object, let the way you photograph it suggest its stature for you. How it really looks isn't important as the way you want it to look. Rather than document the wilderness, be creative with it. *Size* is an analytical term, while *Stature* is more interpretive. Once you've lost a sense of scale, things can be as big as you want them to be. Think of this new-found freedom to change the scale of things as just one more creative tool at your disposal, a way to make your photography as personal as your signature.

PROBLEMS

When taking macrophotographs you will find yourself facing problems which, though not unfamiliar to you, have been intensified because of the closeness of your camera to your subject. They have been discussed in Chapter Four but are worth reiterating here.

Short Depth of Field

The closer you get to your subject, the narrower your field of focus, and macrophotography is as close as you can get. If you use your depth-of-field preview button, you'll see just how small that field of focus really is. As pointed out in Chapter One there are two things your depth-of-field preview button can help you determine: the size of your field of focus, and its placement. A narrow field of focus is not automatically undesirable. Out-of-focus backgrounds can lend a softness to your image, which may be exactly what you want. There are several options to consider if your field is narrower than you desire.

Use a slower shutter speed, so you can increase your f-stop, and consequently your depth of field. (This may cause you to have to use a tripod, or other artificial support.)

Use a faster film, or push the film you've got. With the same lens, subject, shutter speed, and lighting conditions, ASA 400 film allows you to use a smaller aperture than ASA 100 film. This, in turn, allows you to increase your depth of field. If you push your film (e.g. shoot ASA 400 film with your camera set at ASA 800), remember to mark the roll for special processing.

Place your subject in a plane parallel to the plane of your film. If you want both the stem and the front of the cap of a mushroom to be sharp, tilt your camera so they are both approximately the same distance from your lens. In the close-up, head-on position, the cap is usually sufficiently in front of the stem to prevent both of them from being in focus at the same time.

Change the placement of your field of focus by focusing on a spot slightly in front of, or in back of, your main subject. Blurry foregrounds are usually more distracting than blurry backgrounds, so move your field of focus to include your main subject, and what is immediately in front of it, to create what appears to be a larger depth of field. This is especially true when the objects in

When your field of focus is narrow, its placement becomes critical. To avoid foreshortening, get down low. 55 mm macro lens.

front of your main subject are close to it but those behind it are not. Focusing on the center of your subject will clear up the blurry background, so you might as well move your point of focus forward and clear up the foreground.

When selecting your point of focus (i.e. when placing your field of focus), it is important to remember that the relationship between point of focus and depth of field is different for macrophotography. With standard lenses at standard distances the field of focus is generally found to be ⅓ in front of, and ⅔ behind, the point of focus. At macro distances, the point of focus is just about in the middle of the field of focus, with the clear area in front of it being approximately equal to the clear area behind it. Whether you remember this or not, your major concern will still be that your field of focus is extremely shallow. The best way to position it, and thereby make maximum use of the sharp area of your image, is to use your depth-of-field preview button, and see what moving your point of focus actually does to your image.

Low Light

One of the ways to maximize depth of field is to use a smaller aperture, forcing you into using slower shutter speeds. Even if your photographic subject isn't on the dark floor of a dense forest, you will be functioning as though in a low-light situation. This problem is not unique to macrophotography, nor are its solutions.

Use a tripod. By now the association should be automatic. Low light equals slow shutter speeds, and slow shutter speeds equals tripod.

Use a faster film or push the one you've got (see comments in the previous section on short depth of field).

Supplement the existing light by using a strobe or reflectors. A strobe has the advantage of both increasing the amount of light and freezing the action. Most "at the nest" bird photographs are taken this way. If you don't have a strobe, reflectors may provide sufficient supplemental lighting to suit your purpose. All you need is a piece of aluminum foil, a foil-covered sun-bathing reflector, or even a large white card.

A normal lens can be converted to a close-up lens with the addition of a bellows attachment. © 1980 Roy Silverstein.

Camera Shake

At standard distances (with slow shutter speeds) camera shake can be a major problem. At macro distances, it can be devastating. It can be so serious a problem that even using a tripod isn't enough of a precaution. The tripod may be holding the camera steady enough, but sometimes just depressing the shutter can create enough movement to blur your image. There are three things you can do to decrease the chances of camera shake while using a tripod.

Use the camera's self-timer (if you have one) to take the picture for you. The automatic shutter-release mechanism disturbs the camera less than a finger. As you set the timer, be careful not to move the camera, for at macro distances, moving the camera even a fraction of an inch can have a major effect on composition. If you've carefully selected it, you certainly don't want to unconsciously change it.

Use a cable release. Triggering the shutter from a distance has many advantages. You won't be touching the camera, so you don't have to worry about changing the composition of your image. You can back away from the

Portraits in nature aren't limited to wildlife, as this burl illustrates. 55 mm macro lens.

camera, thereby eliminating your shadow from the subject. If setting up your camera forced you into a precarious or uncomfortable position you'll be able to reposition yourself comfortably. Since cables come in a wide range of lengths, you have tremendous flexibility in this area, including photographing nests from a blind several feet away.

Lock up your mirror. If you do everything in your power to eliminate the external causes of camera shake, there is still one internal problem which you may not be aware of when working at a close range. This is the vibrations caused by the mirror's moving up and out of the way at the precise moment the shutter is opened. There is something you can do to stop this internal shake, as long as you don't have to see what is in the viewfinder when photographing. Compose your image, get your camera set to go, and then lock up the mirror before you release the shutter. When you do so you will no longer be able to see through the viewfinder, but if the image is not going to change, you won't have to worry about selecting a new composition. Consider using a strobe when photographing a moving insect on a flower, or waiting for it to get in the perfect position. With a strobe, the photograph is taken in such a short amount of time mirror vibrations are no longer a problem.

Wind

The most frustrating problem of slow-shutter-speed photography is the wind. If you succeed in keeping your camera still, how do you keep the landscape still? At macro distances even a slight breeze can blow flower petals right out of your viewfinder.

If you are photographing close to your base camp or car, construct a wind screen from your supplies. A large piece of plastic doesn't take up much room when packed (and can double as a rain and condensation precaution). Setting up a wind screen is easier if someone helps you hold it. Chances are you won't need a very large screen, considering the size of your subject, and your proximity to it. If you can't construct one, there are other things you can do.

Just as you can use your body to create shade, sometimes you can use your body to shelter your subject from the wind. If all else fails, wait for that split second when the breeze lets up. With fast reactions, you'll probably have sufficient time to get that blur-free image. If you're not sure you got it, take a few more insurance shots.

Manipulating your Tripod

In Chapter Two, we stressed the importance of being familiar with your equipment, of knowing how to manipulate your tripod to take advantage of all its positions quickly in the field. This is more important for macrophotography than any other kind of photography. Even with fluidity and expertise, setting up a tripod is extremely challenging when the subject is two inches away. Nothing can dampen creativity faster than trying to use equipment that doesn't want to cooperate. A tripod can seem to have a mind of its own when you're having difficulties setting it up. Become completely familiar with your tripod in advance, so the only obstacles you have to face are those you find in the field. They'll be plentiful enough: a boulder that's too slippery, ground that's too soft, or a branch that won't let you get close to your subject. Aside from the technical aspects of macrophotography, the challenge of getting both you and your tripod in proper position is enough to make the results rewarding.

Disturbing the Environment

Though positioning yourself, and your tripod, are sufficient challenges for any macrophotographer, try to do so without disturbing the environment. Stretching your body out on the ground to photograph the under side of a mushroom is difficult, but to do so without crushing nearby things seems impossible. Sometimes it is, and this is where the ethics of a wilderness photographer come into play.

Positioning you and your tripod is half the challenge of macrophotography. A mini-tripod can increase your maneuverability. © 1980 Susan Lariviere.

Holding your camera so that the plane of the film is parallel to the plane of the mushrooms makes maximum use of your limited depth of field. 55 mm macro lens.

In the wilderness, unlike in a studio, things aren't always where we'd like them to be. Where do we draw the line between rearranging the environment, and working with what's there? If a blade of grass is growing in front of your subject, should you pull it out? The answer is yes. But, if you want to photograph the top of one mushroom with the bottom of another, do you have the right to pull one out of the ground, and lay it down near the other? This becomes a matter of choice.

Judging from photographs in books about mushrooms, there are photographers who do this all the time. There are others who never do this. How we treat the wilderness is as personal as our photography. Our photography reflects how we relate to the wilderness. To some, the photograph you would have gotten of that mushroom isn't as important as the damage you would have done to the tiny ecosystem surrounding it.

115

Mammoth Hot Springs detail (Yellowstone National Park).
500 mm lens.

7

Roadside and Campground Photography

By now you should have become aware of the importance of slowing down while hiking, of not worrying about making it to a particular destination in record time. There are photographic subjects along the way that may prove to be more interesting than what you find at your final destination, but you won't see these subjects unless you take the time to look for them.

The same is true about rushing to the trail head, or campground, in your car. The road, paved or not, cuts through the same type of environment you'll be hiking in. You can find interesting subjects here, too. If you look carefully, you'll discover that roadside photography isn't limited to panoramas and overlooks.

What kind of subjects can you find while driving your car? Just about everything you can find while hiking: waterfalls, flowers, woods, meadows, sunrises and sunsets, spectacular views. The flora and fauna are often the same as where you will be hiking.

The main difficulty with roadside photography is that it's hard to anticipate just what there is for the taking. It seems unthinkable that any outstanding nature photographs could have been taken alongside the road. Certainly someone had to hike for days to a remote section of the wilderness to find such an unspoiled corner of the natural world. In reality many of the best nature studies exist only a matter of feet from the paved road. But, in truth, people hike through the wilderness after they get there on roads that wind through the same type of landscape. A careful look at the roadside photographs in this book proves one should not wait to explore or shoot.

Besides the fact that you may miss something spectacular, there are two important practical reasons for mastering the techniques of roadside photography. First, and foremost, is comfort and convenience. You have access to every piece of equipment without having to worry about carrying it, or sheltering it from the elements. The second reason is that roadside photography provides you with a rehearsal for your backpacking experience. Since the habitat, climate, and weather will be the same as your hiking area, you'll get a good idea of what lenses, and other pieces of equipment, will be needed. This will help you decide what to pack, and what to leave behind, when leaving the car.

If your time is limited, and you want to see as much of a National Park as possible, roadside photography is definitely worth exploring. You will be able to visit a greater variety of habitats in your car than by hiking just one trail. At Yellowstone National Park, a day's drive can

The roads in National Parks allow you to see a variety of habitats quickly and conveniently, including wildlife which you can photograph from the comfort and safety of your car. (Elk rut, Yellowstone National Park) 200 mm lens.

lead you from geyser basin to pine forest, from open meadow to the Grand Canyon of the Yellowstone, with as interesting a variety of wildlife along the way. Moose, bear, bison, elk, deer, water fowl, and birds of prey can be seen, and photographed, from the comfort and safety of your car.

THE HOW-TO'S OF ROADSIDE PHOTOGRAPHY

Keep your equipment next to you in the car, with the camera bag open and accessible. Know where everything is, so you can find what you are looking for quickly. Have a special place to put your exposed film, so you don't have to sift through it to find a fresh roll, and keep your most-used lens on the camera. Take advantage of the space your car provides to keep lenses and accessories within easy reach. For comfort, and convenience, this is as close as you can get to working in a studio.

As in hiking, there are three problems with taking photographs from your car: keeping your equipment protected from vibrations, dust, and, direct sunlight. In a moving vehicle, all three problems are intensified. Unless you are driving on a super highway, the road will probably be bumpy and dusty. So remember to keep your equipment covered, and cushioned from rattling against each other. As far as the sun is concerned, we have a tendency to forget the damage it can do when we are driving all day with the windows of the car open. Our heads may be shaded from the sun's hot rays, and the wind may be cool, but the roll of film in the camera, or on the back window ledge may be doing a slow burn. It doesn't matter if it is hot or cold outside, keep your film out of the direct rays of the sun.

The best way to increase the probability of finding good photographic subjects is to drive slowly. Most people are in such a rush to get where they're going that they don't know where they've been. In your case, you'll not only know where you've been, but you'll have pictures to prove it. Unlike hiking you're not walking through the woods, you're driving, and that places the extra responsibility on you to operate your vehicle with care.

Sidelighting helps to accentuate the forms of subjects. Drive slowly so that you can tune in to the subtle aspects of nature. 200 mm lens.

One reason for driving slowly is so you can see more of what is around you. Another reason is so that you can stop your car easily when you find something to photograph. The image of someone flying past a roadside waterfall, then slamming on the brakes to bring the car to a skidding, abrupt halt, hardly fits in with the concept of the sensitive tuned-in nature lover. That kind of driving is contradictory to the proper approach to wilderness photography, and more importantly, it's dangerous.

When driving through wilderness areas, tune in to the environment, but also tune in to the other cars. Fast driving is dangerous, even if you don't stop short, but slow driving isn't synonymous with safety. Be aware of cars behind you, for most of them will not be as interested as you in the details of the surroundings. Keep to the right, so they can pass, or pull over in an appropriate spot to let them by. You needn't pull over for every car, but if a string of them piles up behind you pull off the road. Forcing people to pass on winding, narrow roads is extremely dangerous. Getting into an accident, or causing one, is hardly the way to create the comfortable, relaxed atmosphere necessary for creativity.

If you do pass something you want to photograph, and can't immediately stop, keep going until you can find a safe place to turn around. Don't back up, unless it is for a short distance and you are sure there is no one behind you. Keep in mind that other drivers on the road will be moving much faster than you, will not be looking for reasons to stop, and certainly don't expect to find a car stopped on the road, turning around, or backing up. Driving carefully may cost you a little time, but if something is worth stopping for, it will still be there a few minutes later.

Finally, it is important to consider where to stop, or park, your car. Pull completely off the road, so you are not blocking a driving lane, but do so only where it won't damage the roadside. Even in the most remote wilderness areas, roads frequently have areas that are suitable for parking. They may not be exactly where you'd like to park, but they are certainly within walking range.

Parking Your Car: Diversionary Tactics

Parking in designated areas serves another purpose. Most people are tuned in to hiking, and taking photographs, on a trail. Like the subjects of macrophotography, roadside photographic subjects are generally overlooked. Keeping them that way becomes a problem, especially when you are involved in the creative process. One way to not keep a subject secret is to park your car in a conspicuous place. Stopping in the middle of the road creates a "What do they see?" attitude in other drivers, who then stop to find out. Anyone who has been in Yellowstone National Park knows how a bear on the side of the road can cause a traffic jam. In Yellowstone, people often search for wildlife by seeing where cars have stopped. In addition to losing your privacy, you may be causing havoc, for these drivers probably aren't as careful as you, and will park anywhere. If you are photographing wildlife, you may lose more than your privacy, for even the most trusting animal has a limit to the number of noisy cars, screaming children, and snapshooters it can stand. Park in a pull-off, or rest area, and no one will be interested in why you stopped.

The diversionary tactics of roadside photography serve several purposes: to prevent cars from piling up on the side of the road, to keep your work area private, and to keep wildlife subjects from being frightened away. Parking your car where it won't draw attention is only one such tactic. The others also aim to draw people's attention away from what you are really doing. Have friends sit next to the car, so that it looks as if you just got tired of driving and decided to take a rest. If you have more than one camera, have one set up on a tripod, so that it points at something totally uninteresting. As careful as you may be, don't be surprised if someone sorts through all these decoys, and zeroes in on your subject. Some people have amazing amounts of curiosity, and perserverance, especially when it comes to taking photographs.

Wildlife Photography: Your Car as a Blind

The greatest contribution your car can provide to roadside photography is its use as a blind. Wildlife that nests and feeds near a highway is used to cars, so approach them correctly, and you'll get your photographs. There are just a few things to remember when using your car as a blind.

First, don't stop right where they are. If you are traveling at highway speeds this won't be a problem, for by the time you realize you want to shoot you'll be sufficiently past your subject. After you come to a stop, turn around slowly and carefully and return to the location as quietly as possible, so as not to frighten the wildlife. Every animal reacts differently to encroachment, and the amount of space each one requires before it feels threatened is not easy to determine. If you approach slowly, you might be able to get closer than a fast-moving vehicle would ever be allowed. If the road permits turning your car around, let the angle of the sun determine which side of your subject you approach from.

Wildlife along the highways is accustomed to cars and won't be disturbed if you approach carefully. At any moment, though, be prepared to see it flee. (Snowy egret, Everglades National Park, Florida) 500 mm mirror lens.

Once you've parked near your subject, take some telephoto shots of it through the open window of your car. Rest the barrel of your lens on the partially open glass, using a soft shirt, hat, or bean bag, to cushion the vibrations. If your angle is right, you may want to set up your tripod, using the car door as a blind and shooting through the open window. When you open the door, do so slowly and quietly. A door that's opened too quickly can make a loud thud, or create a flash of reflecting sunlight, both of which can easily frighten wildlife.

Remember to be extremely conscious of how you set up your tripod, for it's very easy to create a tremendous amount of clatter, and clunking noises. With a racket like that, it won't matter if you are using your doors as a blind or not.

Consider getting closer to the subject only after you have taken all the desired telephoto and wide-angle dis-

With your car as a blind, you'll be able to get excellent portraits of roadside wildlife. (Great Blue Heron, Everglades National Park, Florida) 500 mm mirror lens.

tance shots. Let the car roll a little, or get out, and inch up on foot, but be prepared to see your subject flee at any moment. The closer you get, the greater the probability of flight.

Wildlife photography from your car: the safety factor

One of the greatest advantages of taking wildlife photographs from your car is safety, both for you and your subjects. That you feel safer is not hard to understand. Anyone would feel more comfortable meeting a bear while inside a car than while hiking on a trail. Since you feel safe, you're free to concentrate on photography, and the possible exciting images. What makes them especially exciting is that they won't look as though they were taken from a car. Close-ups of a bear will look as though you were dangeriously close to the bear.

The safety element of a car works both ways, for wildlife won't feel threatened, and when your subject is secure it will pose for the camera. Just remember to keep the car and the road out of the picture, and thus preserve the natural-habitat appearance of the image.

There is one common pitfall to roadside photography. If you are like most photographers, the moment a good subject catches your eye, your attention is focused on it alone. You think about lenses, and composition, and where to park your car. Even as you park, your eyes are pinned to your distant subjects. But, before you get out of your car, carefully scan your immediate surroundings, be conscious of possible hazards, such as poison oak, or snakes in the grass. Don't step blindly out of your car into tall brush, or onto a pile of rocks. A herd of elk is a compelling sight, and you won't want to take your eyes off them for a minute, but if you're smart you will long enough to be sure of you.

An example of this comes to mind when thinking about Florida's Everglades National Park. During the drier seasons, the drain pipes that run under the road usually still have free-flowing water. Because of this, there are fish and fish eaters, such as egrets, herons, ibises, and wood storks nearby. It's an excellent place to photograph plumed birds, but be careful about getting out of your car.

Roadside Photography, though not limited to dramatic vistas, does include some spectacular ones. (Monument Valley, Arizona) 28 mm lens.

The roads in wilderness areas take you through the same type of habitat you'll be hiking through, so you needn't wait until you're on the trail to take pictures. (Mt. Baker, Washington)

Drain pipes are also excellent places to find alligators. They're quiet, and hard to spot, and since you probably haven't taken your eyes off the egret you've got the makings of a very dangerous situation. Take photographs from inside your car, and don't get out unless you are absolutely sure it is safe. If you're wondering whether there's an alligator sleeping inside a drain pipe, assume that there is, and don't get out of your car.

The best way to master roadside photography is to let someone else do the driving. This way, you can concentrate on looking for subjects, while the driver worries about the road and other cars. With two sets of eyes, you'll see more, and will be more able to manipulate your equipment. Take photographs from the right window while the car is moving, or from the road while your companion watches for approaching vehicles and waves them passed. It's easier, and a lot more fun if you have friend with you.

A discussion of roadwide photography should not be limited to cars, for it can be practiced just as easily from a bicycle or motorcycle. The equipment packing, parking, and safety requirements are different (one does not have the protection of a car), but the experience can be just as rewarding. The biker has a tremendous advantage by being more exposed to the elements, while a passenger in a car can feel encapsulated. A biker doesn't have the same worries as people in cars. No matter how you are travelling, you'll probably be spending more time driving than hiking. Try and make the drive just as enjoyable as the photographic experience.

CAMPGROUND PHOTOGRAPHY

Campground photography is midway between roadside photography and trail photography. As in roadside photography, you have access to your equipment without having to carry it. As in hiking, your freedom of movement isn't restricted by your car. Established campgrounds are generally in attractive settings, usually near water, and offer opportunities for photography similar to those in the surrounding wilderness. Good nature photographs aren't

Redwoods, Prairie Creek, Redwood National Park, California. 28 mm lens.

always taken on a trail. Campground photography, like roadside photography, is one more way to make maximum use of your wilderness experience.

Comfort and Convenience

In the campground you have access to all your equipment, whether it is spread out on the seat of your car, on the floor of your tent, or on the picnic table in the shade. Because of this freedom you can function as if you were in a studio. Set up two cameras with different types of film. Use pieces of equipment you don't take with you on the trail, and lenses that you infrequently use. You'll have a wonderful opportunity to experiment with a variety of equipment at your disposal, and a comfortable environment. Fatigue is the number one damper on creativity, but in the campground you won't have to contend with inclining trails, slippery footing, and heavy packs. You'll be able to concentrate entirely on your photography.

Time

Another factor that affects creativity is time. If you are rushing to get to a certain destination, or trying to keep up with companions, you won't be able to enjoy your photographic experience. There won't be time to truly attune to the wilderness, to experience where you are hiking, to find photographic subjects to experiment with your equipment, or to create the best images. The campground is one of those places where no time pressures seem relevant. You're not rushing to get somewhere, you're already there, and your companions are nearby. By reducing pressures, you increase your ability to be creative.

Taking photographs in the campground increases the amount of time you actually spend on your photography. Time that would ordinarily be lost can be used constructively. Take pictures while you wait for your companions to get ready, while you wait for the fire to get hot, or for the water to boil. If you only take photographs on the trail, you'll be eliminating a great deal of the time you actually spend in the wilderness.

"Fall Birch." Colors are saturated and blue sky darkened with the use of a polarizing filter. The brightness of the tree against these colors provides contrast. (Paper birch, New England) 28mm lens Kodachrome 25.

Above left. "Moss Stream." Composing the image with both bright, dappled sunlit areas and darker areas is extremely important. If you have a depth-of-field preview button, close your lens down, press the button, and look through the viewfinder. Kodachrome 25 85mm lens ½ sec. at f/16. Left. "Mushroom." Changing your perspective with familiar subjects helps you to explore new visions. A 55mm macro lens was used in available light at about four inches from the subject with Kodachrome 64. Above. "Snowy Egret." Framing the subject with subtle, out-of-focus background tones creates visual attention. Extreme quiet and patience must be exercised in photographing wildlife. (Snowy Egret, Florida Everglades) 500mm lens with Ektachrome 400.

"Opal Lake." A unique change in weather with contrasting lighting conditions can contribute to dramatic landscapes. To capture these moments, speed in deciding on lens and composition is required. (Yellowstone National Park) 28mm lens. Kodacolor II.

Below. "Florida Panther." A long telephoto lens can provide visual intimacy with a difficult subject. (Florida Panther, Southern Florida) 1000mm lens with Ektachrome 400 and a tripod were the tools for this image. Right. "Monta Rosa." Mountain photography need not be pursued solely with a wide-angle lens. Early morning light, high in ultra-violet, polarizer and a 200mm lens recorded this glacial scene. Below, right. "Berry." To make your subject more dominant, framing it with a darker background reduces distractions. (Salmonberry, Mt. Baker, Washington State) Bright early morning sun with a bellows, tripod, 50mm lens and Ektachrome 400 were used.

"Flower falls." Bright, overcast days can create subdued colors. Slow shutter speeds convey motion and small apertures maximize depth of field. Kodachrome II with 55mm macro lens and a tripod were used.

In the campground, you can take photographs at times when you wouldn't be on the trail. Night time shot of spider in web taken with strobe. 55 mm macro lens.

Lighting

Taking photographs in your campground makes it easier to take advantage of the most spectacular light in which to work—the early morning, and the late afternoon. At these times you can get the longest shadows, the greatest contrast, and with a polarizing filter, the bluest skies. Just minutes from your bed, you can find early morning dew, and misty sunrises. It's easier than rising early to see them from the trail. In the evening you can take pictures until the sun's rays are gone, and not worry about hiking back to

Since campground subjects are so accessible, you can wait until the lighting is just right for your composition. 28 mm lens.

camp in the dark. It's not difficult to get early-morning and late-afternoon photographs from a trail. It's just easier to get them from the campground, because that's where you usually are at those times of day.

Lazy Days and Inclement Weather

No matter how serious your involvement, your interest in both hiking and photography will fluctuate. Some days you'll be first to break camp. Other days you'll feel as though you could never get out of the campground. Times like that are perfect for campground photography. Take a leisurely stroll around the grounds, and examine the flowers and plants, or experiment with macrophotography. On a day when you don't feel like doing very much, it's amazing how much can be accomplished taking pictures in the campground.

Then there are days when the weather makes hiking uninviting: cold, rainy, damp, and dreary days. At those times, photography around the campsite keep your creativity level high. During this kind of weather, you won't be out on a long hike, and can come back to shelter to warm up, dry off, change clothes, or eat, and then go back out again. You needn't carry your full pack, so moving around will be easier. You won't be negotiating difficult trails, thus making the weather less bothersome. On days when the trail is uninviting, let the campground be your photographic playground.

With all the comforts of your campsite nearby, the season's first snowflakes needn't put a damper on your creativity. The snowflakes on this bracket fungus add contrast to the composition. 55 mm macro lens.

Your Most Meaningful Photos

One of the things about a campsite is that it will soon develop a feeling of home. It is your home away from home, and as such you probably would like some photographs to remind you what it looked like, where it was, and what you experienced there. This is especially true if you're there with friends. If you hike different trails during the day, this may be the only place where you are all together. Early morning meals, late night campfires, offer opportunities for photographing the inter-personal aspects of your wilderness experience. What you share with your companions will be part of your memories, so make it part of your photographs as well.

What to photograph

Everyone is aware of the typical "let's go camping" magazine photos: people, campfires, smoke in the pines, breaking camp, cooking meals, waking up at dawn. Your subjects needn't be campers, tents, and trailers unless you want them to be. Whether you are sleeping overnight on the trail, or in an established campground full of cars, a fine sampling of the flora will surround you. Due to the clearing operations necessary to construct more formal campgrounds, certain types of plants are more accessible. Berries, flowers, nurse logs, ferns, moss, mushrooms, and pine cones, all have something special to offer.

Within a campground, each campsite is a little bit different. They may all have the same picnic table and barbeque grill, but if you've ever watched how long it takes some people to pick one out, you'll understand that they aren't all the same. The differences are more than the distance of the bathroom or the location of the water. Even in an empty campground, people search for the site that feels just right. Each one has a slightly different orientation, and arrangement of flora. With nature as exterior decorator, the selection of a site is made after a great deal of consideration, even on a subconscious level.

Shrubs aren't the only attraction in a campground. Wildlife can be found coming for water and food. Since they are used to people in this environment, they generally

Wildlife that is accustomed to people in the campgrounds will usually stay close enough for you to get intimate portraits with a telephoto lens. (Red shouldered hawk, southern Florida) 500 mm mirror lens.

come closer than they would on the trail. Birds and chipmunks are perennial favorites, but sometimes deer and bear show up. Since campgrounds have been partially cleared, you'll have a better angle to photograph from, and lots of props to help you. Stand on a picnic table, or on top of your car, to see over the brush. Don't worry about making noise. Wildlife that frequents campgrounds is used to the commotion their visits cause.

Campground photography can be enjoyed on many levels—when you're serious about your photography and want to spend hours exploring with your macro lens, when you don't want to do very much but stay close to camp, when you want to take photographs of good times

Campground habitats are as varied as the surrounding wilderness and offer just as many photographic opportunities. (Arches National Park, Utah) 28 mm lens.

with friends, when you want to save moments only shared by you and the raindrops. There are quiet and hectic times, but there are always people, wildlife, flowers, and trees. The campsite is not just a place to return to when the photographic day is over.

Your images can capture the vast range of experiences that are collectively called camping. Photographs need not appear as though they were composed in the campground, for the image of a berry will not show the picnic table near it. You have a chance to actually improve on the wilderness, for the images you take home will contain none of the imperfections of the places where they were made. The surrounding environment suggested by your images, and created in the minds of those who see them, may be far more beautiful than it actually was. You may have photographed a part of the natural world, but in creating an image you have also created a new and far more exciting world—the world of one's imagination. It's no wonder that people look at campground, or roadside, images and can't believe such beauty could exist anywhere but in the most remote regions of the wilderness. Good nature photographs create a world of their own.

Like roadside images, photographs taken in a campground needn't look as though they were quite so accessible. (Great Blue Heron, Everglades, Florida) 200 mm lens.

Cliff detail. (Zion National Park, Utah) 200 mm lens.

8

Photographic Themes

Your first contact with photography was probably like most people's: photographs taken of friends and relatives to record a special event, or photographs taken on vacations to preserve the memories of these times. Everyone was involved in these photographs the same way, and everyone knew why the photographs were being taken, but very little thought was given to how the pictures could be better.

As your interest in photography grew you acquired new equipment, not just a point-and-shoot camera, and you became a serious photographer. Your camera was no longer a mere recorder of the fleeting moments in your life. It became a creative tool, and as a creator you were faced with new problems: what to photograph, and how to do it well. Suddenly your photography had to have a purpose, and seemed more important than the snapshots you used to take. The purpose of those snapshots was clear, but what purpose do your photographs serve now?

The answer, of course, is a very personal one. It needn't be very different from the purpose of your previous snapshots, but the images should be better. Don't let the range of flexibility your sophisticated equipment provides turn your portfolio into a chaotic assortment of random images. To improve your photography, to create a portfolio with cohesiveness and a sense of style, you have to become conscious of the goal of your photography. Why do you take pictures and what do you want them to say?

These questions are of primary concern when working on a photographic theme. You may be compiling images for a photo essay, working on assignment, or using a theme as an exercise to expand your creative potential. No matter what your reason for getting involved in it, theme photography is very different from the birthday and graduation snapshots you used to take.

Photographic themes can develop before, during, or after the fact. You can start a photographic excursion with a theme in mind (*before*), see one develop spontaneously as you photograph (*during*), or find one lacing through your photographs as you organize the images for presentation purposes (*after*). Since the first two affect your wilderness experience, they are worth studying in detail.

BEFORE: THE PHOTO ASSIGNMENT

The most important questions to be answered when beginning a photo assignment are: "Why photograph that particular subject?" "What's so interesting about it?" "What do you want to show photographically?" An in-depth study is more than a collection of random, unclear, and undirected images. If you have no goals, or purpose, to your theme your images will be as undirected as you are.

When selecting a theme, make sure it isn't too broad (e.g., birds of North America vs. birds of prey). With a broad topic it's much harder to be cohesive. You will need a large number of photographs to cover your topic well, and maybe too large a number for the project to be really practical.

Once you've selected your subject, it's important to know what you want to say about it, and what you want to convey through your images. Your images are a vehicle for relaying a message, and you have to know what that message is. Do not just go out, and shoot everything you see, hoping that your images will determine it for you. The old adage is "One picture is worth 1000 words." You shouldn't need 1000 pictures to help you find those words.

Make a list of what you hope to accomplish photographically: what images are absolutely essential to your

There are many factors that determine what we'll find in the wilderness and that in turn affects what we end up photographing. 28 mm lens.

story, what you hope to shoot, what's worth coming back for, and what's worth waiting for.

Decide where you have to go, and when, to capture the images. Will it be different geographical areas, different habitats, the zoo, different seasons, different times of the day, or different weather conditions?

What equipment do you need: tripod, strobe, reflector, rain gear, wind screen, or blind. What film, and special accessories will be needed?

Be flexible, for things may not go as expected, and the final images may be very different from the ones you thought you'd get. Your whole approach, or theme, may change once you are in the field. If it does, fine, for that means you are responding to your environment, to what you've found, rather than looking for what you thought you'd find. Hopefully you haven't limited your flexibility by only bringing your macro lens or your wide-angle. Remember to be prepared for anything, especially the unexpected.

Above all, don't be boring. Vary your perspective, your lenses, your approach. Include habitat, and different lighting conditions, etc. Decide whether or not you want to include yourself in the story.

There are lots of things to consider when setting out on a photographic assignment, but it all comes back to the basics: the purpose of the exercise, and the aim of the story. This will tell you what to cover and how. There are many different approaches to photographic themes, and many different treatments of subjects. The important thing is that there be some element that ties it all together, something that makes it cohesive. The *what* may be the thread, or the *how* or the *when*, with the elements in harmony, or

Vary your approach. There are many different ways to personalize your wilderness photographs. 55 mm macro lens.

in contrast. Some examples are listed below to give you an idea of the range of themes and treatments awaiting your creative interpretation.

> Everglades Wildlife
> Abstracts in Nature
> Trees
> Waterfalls and Streams
> Mushrooms
> The Seasons
> The Coastline
> The Desert
> The Forest Floor
> Mountains

DURING: SPONTANEOUS THEME DEVELOPMENT

"Good nature photographs seem to come in groups. Whether it be trees, or waterfalls, each year ends with a bountiful crop of one particular subject, as though nature endowed these elements with exceptional beauty, and placed them in unusual abundance in our path. It may be that photographers become highly sensitive to those elements, thereby discovering them more frequently, but whatever the reason, this year, for us, was the year of the mushroom."   *Reprinted by permission of the Sierra Club.*

Whether your trail diary has a similar entry or not, you've probably reached a similar conclusion at some time in your photographic experience. It may have been the year of the mushroom, or the year of the tree, or the month of something else, but themes do frequently present themselves once we are in the field. There are three basic explanations for this phenomenon.

The first is that it may very well have been a good year for mushrooms, trees, or flowers. Seasons change, the climate varies, and some years are noticeably drier or wetter than others. The amount of precipitation, the mildness of the winter, the smoothness of the transition to spring, all these are factors that determine what we'll find in the wilderness.

Alpine wildflowers, for example, have a short growing period. The best time to spot them depends on the alti-

142

tude, climate, and amount of snowfall that year. What may be a good time for flowers one year may not be a good time the next.

The second reason is a heightened sensitivity to your subjects which increases your ability to perceive them. There really aren't any more plants or flowers than there were the year before. You just notice them more.

The final reason is that the searching itself becomes a learning experience. The more you look, the more you find. The more you find, the more you know where to look. Your searching becomes reinforced in places where you expected to find your subjects, and intermittently reinforced in places where you didn't. This is especially true when searching for elusive subjects, whether they be plants or wildlife. The challenge of locating them makes the emotion of finding the subjects so much stronger. There's an excitement to this kind of photographic experience that very quickly crowds all other subjects out of your field of interest, then your field of view. As your ability to locate your subjects increases, your interest in locating other subjects decreases.

At first this may seem contradictory to the intent of the photographer's approach to hiking. How can you increase your awareness of your surroundings if you narrow your field of concentration? Although working on a theme seems to create tunnel vision, there are two very broadening side effects to this photographic exercise.

The most immediate benefit of working on a theme is that you can enjoy nature from a new perspective. In searching for your subject you invariably see other things as well. You get a better understanding of the interrelationships between various aspects of nature, for while you are studying your subject you are also studying the ecosystem in which it lives. As our trail diary indicates:

"Our pace was slow, our senses keen, for we feared the careless step that could destroy the subjects for which we searched. We did discover more mushrooms this way, and other things as well, for we were far more sensitive to the feel of the earth beneath us: the crunching of pungent pine needles, the cushioning of the water-laden spongy moss."   Reprinted by permission of the Sierra Club.

You may be narrowing your field of vision, but you are also increasing your concentration on the subject, consequently increasing the depth of your understanding. You may be studying only mushrooms, but you gather knowledge from the experience.

What will you learn? Certainly if you study mushrooms you will learn what they look like, and where they grow. You will also learn about what grows near them, what's part of their immediate ecosystem. You'll gain an understanding of the interdependence of nature, of the rules that govern survival in that habitat. You're studying the world of mushrooms, but also more, for this habitat is a microcosm of nature itself. Study one part of nature in depth, and you'll end up with a better understanding of nature as a whole.

The second benefit of working on a theme is its effect on your photography, specifically on your creative potential. One of the suggestions made in Chapter Four is to vary your position, and the lenses you use on a given subject. Look through your portfolio, or collection of slides. I'm sure you'll find some wide-angle, mid-range, telephoto and some macro shots. It looks like a good variety of images, but let's take a closer look at how you treat individual subjects.

Are all your images of mountains and trees wide-angle shots? Are your flowers and mushrooms all macro close-ups? Are your images too cliché? Ask yourself if your photographs are similar to all your other images, or created in the style of other photographers. If they are, then working on a theme is a perfect exercise for you.

Since you're not changing your subject, working on a specific theme forces you to vary your treatment of that subject. If you didn't, you'd very quickly get bored with shooting the same thing over and over again, in the same way with the same lens. To keep your excitement and interest high, change lenses, and this will change your perspective. You will begin to see your subject differently, and that increases your creative potential. As you experiment with different lenses and different perspectives, you'll discover what you are capable of doing to improve the quality and collection of your images.

With a purpose in mind, the energy required for both hiking and photography are channeled in the same direction. Your destinations and time limitations are set by you, as opposed to being imposed by some outside determinant. You finally achieve a true blending of the backpacking and photographic experiences.

Working on themes can help you improve your photographic technique, expand your creative potential, and give you better insight into the nature of a photographic statement. It can increase your awareness of your surroundings, thereby affecting your hiking and photographic experiences, and can give you a sense of purpose which increases your enjoyment of both. Best of all, it can extend the excitement you feel beyond the wilderness, into the homes, galleries, and publications that will later show your images.

Working on themes brings you back to the basics. Why *do* you take pictures, and *what* do you want them to do? If you want them to go beyond your scrapbook, themes will open the doors for your photography to enter a new, and exciting, world.

No matter what theme you work on, or why you work on it, you'll have an opportunity to expand your vision, your creativity and your understanding of the nature of a photographic statement. (Rainbow, Grand Canyon of the Yellowstone) 28 mm lens.

California Condor soaring above the Tehachapie Mountains, California. 50-300 mm zoom.

9

You And The Wilderness

The backpacking photography experience is unique, and requires proper preparation, and maintenance, of your body as well as your equipment. You'll be doing a lot of bending, squatting, kneeling, and sitting, not to mention walking with a sizeable amount of paraphernalia. It is important for your muscles, your cardiovascular system, and your creativity that you get in shape for the physical stresses ahead. Wear the right clothing and shoes, and learn how to efficiently carry, and move, with your equipment. If your leg muscles tire, or your feet get sore, or your breathing and pulse accelerate to an uncomfortable pace, you won't be able to function in the field. Your creativity will suffer first, and then eventually your desire to take photographs.

Keep your camera accessible, for it's tiring to remove your pack all the time. Check and repair those hot spots on your feet as soon as you feel them. Don't wait for them to turn into blisters. Bring the proper clothing (shirts, hat, gloves, socks, etc.) to decrease your chances of having to deal with hypothermia, heat stroke, heat exhaustion, and rain- or snow-drenched clothes. Carry a snakebite kit with you, and know how to use it. If there is the slightest possibility of your getting injured, or lost, in a remote area, carry a topographical map and some emergency gear, such as a space blanket, matches, small flashlight, and extra food.

Another element of personal safety comes to mind when photographing wildlife. Outstanding wildlife photographs are exciting to see, and if we are to believe the impression made by numerous magazines, and camera advertisements, can be taken by just about anyone. The average amateur photographer honestly believes that he can get as good a picture as the one he saw in a magazine. All he has to do is get close enough.

This thinking is not only wrong; it's dangerous. Though the magazine captions may tell you what lens, *f*-stop, and shutter speed were used, they never tell you *how* the photo was taken—how far the photographer was from the subject, and whether there were any safety elements, such as a blind, a moat, a cage, or a fence. With proper placement, and selection of lens and depth of field, even the most glaring wire fence can be obliterated from a photograph. A maximum-security zoo shot can appear to have been taken in the wild, and a telephoto lens can yield intimate close-ups of subjects far too dangerous to approach. Yet without any knowledge of how those photographs were taken, people in the wilderness constantly try to duplicate the results, endangering themselves, and the wildlife. It is important to remember to keep your distance. If your lens isn't long enough to make the animal large enough in your viewfinder, you'll just have to do without the photograph. When as close as you should be isn't close enough, remember your safety is more important than a picture.

Park rangers are full of stories of people who jeopardize their lives for a picture. They usually have been misled by television's romanticism of wildlife. There's the boy sneaking up on bison grazing in an open field because he wanted to get closer. The girl crouching down at the water's edge to get a close-up of the alligator "sleeping" in the water less than six feet away. The family that smeared honey on a child's face so they could get a picture of a bear licking it off.

People who photograph wildlife for a living don't take foolish chances. Their preparations to protect themselves, and their subjects, is as extensive as any of their other preparations. The truly professional part, which for the amateur is the unfortunate part, is that none of those safety precautions come across in the photograph: no distance, no blind, no fence, just photographer, and subject. If you think about it you'll realize it is precisely because of these careful preparations, and safety barriers, that such photographs are possible. The animal appears the way it does in the photo because it didn't feel threatened, or disturbed, by the photographer. Successful wildlife photography involves many things, but one of the most important, for your sake, and the animal's, is to not take chances with safety.

A final word on safety in the wilderness. Just because you are concentrating on what you want to photograph don't forget to watch where you are going. It's easy to turn an ankle on a rocky or slippery path. In many areas rattlesnakes are a problem, and it's amazing how many people walk the trails in sandals, or other open shoes. Rattlesnakes are not afraid to cross heavily traveled paths, and need little provocation to strike at a rapidly approaching foot. Be careful when hiking in dry rocky areas, and never put your hand or foot in a hole to help you climb unless you know what's inside it. Even if you are careful, and observant, a thick high pair of hiking boots is good extra protection.

PHOTOGRAPHING WILDLIFE

Though wildlife photography is a large enough topic to have a book all its own, there are three basic principles worth mentioning here, because they apply to wilderness photography in general.

Preparation

Know what to look for, where and when to look for it, and be ready to shoot at any time. If you are hiking in a wildlife area, your telephoto or zoom lens should be on your camera, not your wide-angle or macro lens. If you have only a few frames left to your film, load a fresh roll. With wildlife, you'll usually want to take a series of several shots, and unlike portrait-studio subjects, bears and birds may

149

not be around long enough for you to take two shots, rewind, reload, and get set up again. The few frames lost by rewinding in advance will be more than made up for by those special extra shots you will get on your new roll.

Anticipation

Be aware of what your subject is doing, and what it is about to do. If an elk is moving across a field, focus just ahead of it, and let it move into your frame. This is a lot easier than panning, focusing, and composing all at the same time. Look for possible interactions between subjects: greetings, confrontations, and courtship displays. If you wait until you see things happen, it will be too late to photograph them.

Patience

Another one of the unfortunate side effects of wildlife programs on television is that you are led to believe that spending a single hour in the woods will enable you to see your subject run through its entire behavioral repertoire. On television, you do, but that one hour of programming represents weeks and months of filming and editing. It didn't all happen as conveniently as the final product suggests. If you want good wildlife photographs, you have to be willing to wait for them. Stay by a nest, for when the parent bird returns to feed its young you'll get your shot. Watch those grazing stags a little longer, for an elk rut is as exciting to see as it is to photograph.

FIELD COURTESY

Once you appreciate how difficult it is to locate and work with a good photographic subject, you will understand the basis for the kind of interaction that takes place between working professionals in the field. It is not uncommon to come across other people taking photographs on your trail, nor is it difficult to size up the intensity of their involvement. There are three basic rules of courtesy if you see someone working on the trail.

Approach slowly, and quietly, so as not to frighten away his or her subject.

Rather than ask what they are shooting, look to see where the camera is pointed, and let that answer your question. There might be some wildlife hidden in the bushes your voice will frighten away, or the photographer might be too engrossed in the creative process to be disturbed by conversation at that moment.

If you are interested in what is being photographed, stand by quietly, and if the photographer is interested in sharing the subject with you, he or she will let you know. Don't set up your equipment until you feel the other person is finished, and is about to move on, or that he is willing to share his discovery with you.

There's an unwritten sense of possession which develops in the field. It's due in part to the difficulties finding the perfect subject, but also has to do with respecting other photographers' working space. It's difficult to function when there are people getting in your way, or disturbing your concentration. It is only through field courtesy that you will be able to discover the warmth and camaraderie of photographers in the field.

PROBLEMS IN WILDERNESS PHOTOGRAPHY

The wilderness is not a studio, the conditions under which you work cannot be controlled. You cannot regulate the lighting, the temperature, the humidity, or the choice, and placement of your subjects. But, as has been pointed out, you do have some control over what you photograph, and how you photograph it. The following problems are familiar to the experienced wilderness photographer.

Lighting

False meter readings can be due to dappled sunlight, reflections off water or snow, or backlighting while shooting up into the forest's canopy. Use a polarizing filter to reduce glare, or use your own shadow to create a work area with consistent lighting.

Subjects

Unlike the studio photographer, the wilderness photographer has to work with what's there, but by careful selection of position and lens you can increase your variety of photographic images. Remember the wildlife you find is not a captive audience. Be prepared, and capture the moment as it comes. The lack of control over your environment will more than be made up for by the excitement of natural habitat photography

Weather Conditions

Extreme Cold. Frigid weather can cause frostbite, numb fingers, cold metal that sticks to exposed skin, and the feeling of being cold on the outside, and sweaty on the inside. Equipment can be effected by weak batteries, false meter readings, and brittle film that breaks. Static electricity creates "lightning" streaks on the film as it moves across the pressure plate, moveable parts stick because of frozen lubricants, and lenses fog up from breath condensation.

Extreme Heat. High temperatures can cause exhaustion, sunstroke, dehydration, and an accelerating pulse. A general loss of energy is felt, and a desire to avoid carrying heavy gear and photography equipment.

GENERAL TIPS FOR BETTER IMAGES

Use a variety of lenses

Using one lens all the time is a good exercise to heighten your awareness of yours, and your equipment's, capabilities, but a portfolio or scrapbook of all short-telephoto shots is exceedingly boring. Vary your lenses, and vary the lenses you use on specific subjects. Small objects needn't all be macro closeups (try including the surrounding habitat), and panoramas needn't all be photographed with wideangle lenses.

Use a variety of perspectives

Shoot down on things, or up from underneath. Then shoot head on, and from behind. For people and wildlife try profiles, and semi-profiles, showing them approaching and moving away. Unusual photographs require seeing things in a variety of ways.

Vary the lighting

Standing with the sun behind you gives the brightest colors, and is easier to set exposures than when shooting into the sun. There is also much to be said for the dramatic qualities of side lighting, soft backlighting, and silhouetting. All three place a strong emphasis on the shape of your subjects. The ability to perceive the separateness of your subjects, one from the other, or each from the background is an important aspect of visual impact.

Remember, that shooting at different times of the day changes the colors in the sky and sunlit objects, as well as the length and position of the shadows. You may want to incorporate shadows, waiting until they are long enough to fall in a more suitable place, or to wait until the setting sun adds more red to the color of the environment.

Lighting is not synonymous with placement of the sun. Though bright sunlight has the advantages of allowing you to use faster shutter speeds, and to get the crisp, rich color rendition of slower ASA films (such as Kodachrome 25), outstanding images can still be made on cloudy, hazy, and even rainy days. Admittedly, sunlight produces shadows which can enhance the drama of your image, but dappled sunlight, the kind that filters through the canopy of a forest, can make hot spots in streams and wreak havoc with your light meter. On a bright, overcast day, you won't have metering problems, but rather a soft, even lighting flattering to faces, and rich, saturated colors flattering to leaves, flowers, and berries.

Vary the time of day

You will be varying more than just the lighting. There is wildlife in the woods, and even if all you get to see is ground squirrels and birds, you'll find different levels, and types, of activity through the course of the day. Early morning, and just at sundown are usually best for shooting feeding activities, or bathing and drinking at the local water supply. Dew drops, and early-morning frost are exciting to work with, especially since they don't last long. The rising sun warms the earth quickly and in a matter of minutes those glistening crystals can melt and evaporate, rising with the mist. There are special moments to capture all through the day, so vary your hiking and shooting time, and make your photography more enjoyable.

Vary the season

Return to favorite trails, for the wilderness is full of contrasts, from season to season, and year to year. Hike over old paths again, and you'll undoubtedly find what photographically appears to be a new trail. You've changed, your sensitivities are different, and the wilderness has changed, too. Many things affect the natural environment: the lighting, the humidity, the temperature, the precipitation. All these elements change on a daily, as well as a seasonal, basis. Where one year you may find a stream with alpine flowers, the next year you may find a drift of snow. Rushing springtime streams can become trickling brooks in fall. Leaves change both color and size, thickening, and then thinning the canopy of the deciduous forest. Mushrooms can push up through a mossy carpet one week, and be withered to dust the next. Retrace your steps and see what has, or has not, happened to your previously photographed subjects. You can truly appreciate the ephemeral quality of most of nature's creations, and the very special role the photographer can play in preserving a moment of time.

THE WILDERNESS EXPERIENCE

To the snapshot, or scrapbook, photographer hiking without a camera is not very different from hiking with one. He may stop occasionally to take a picture or two, but can quickly catch up to his hiking companions. The serious photographer has a very different kind of wilderness experience, the most obvious contrast being in the amount of time he spends on his photography. It takes time to locate good subjects, time to determine angle and composition, time to experiment with the equipment, and time to decide the photographic statement.

When photographing the wilderness, there will always be great pressure to move on to new subjects. There is an excitement to the outdoors, a lure of the unknown, that constantly draws one further along the trail.

Most trails in National Parks are designed with a particular destination in mind; a lake, rock formation, waterfall, or scenic point. Whether it be one mile, or ten miles to a site, the mere fact that it has been set aside as a point of interest makes it seem terribly important.

The longer the trail, the more stupendous the final destination is expected to be, but after a hard hike it is impossible for anything to be as fantastic as one's expectations demand. Therefore, always look for things to enjoy on the trail, every step of the way. Find your own points of interest, or you will be putting undue pressure on your destination to measure up to your expectations.

Photographing wildlife adds more pressures and frustrations, for you are dealing with more variables and unknowns. The amount of time at your disposal, or what you will be able to photograph, will not be determined solely by yourself. You have less control over the situation, and the behavioral patterns and movements, of your subjects. The sheer unpredictability of wildlife makes it harder to decide if you should remain, or move up the trail. When confronted with the question of leaving a subject, for any reason, consider the following.

Photographic Possibilities

Some things are probable, and therefore worth waiting for. Others are improbable, and are only worth waiting for if you have nothing else to do. Some things you can leave, and come back to. Some things you can't.

Try all angles

Vary your perspective, lenses, and position. Only when you feel you have covered the subject to the best of your abilities should you move on.

Understand Your Images

It doesn't matter what's waiting ahead, if you feel that the situation, or your photographs are terrific. It's easy to stay when you have found something unusual, or when just shooting and experiencing your subject is exciting. Don't worry about shooting one frame, or a hundred, or using one lens or all of them. Move on when you feel you have a fantastic image.

Should you stay or move on? If you're enjoying what you're photographing it doesn't matter what's up ahead on the trail. If you feel good about what you've accomplished, you don't mind moving on. (Anhinga, Everglades National Park, Florida) 50-300 mm zoom at about 250 mm.

The wilderness is there for you to work with. The limits of what you can do are up to you. (Alpine meadow, the height country.) 55 mm macro lens.

Use a hiking companion as a scout

The hardest part about staying is the fact that unless you've seen what's up ahead, you'll never be sure that you made the right decision. The thought that there is something better to photograph tugs at your consciousness and interferes with your ability to concentrate on your craft. You can't be in two places at once, so let a friend check out the rest of the trail. This is especially useful in a densely populated wildlife area, such as Florida's Everglades National Park, where a stroll on the boardwalk reveals something exciting every few hundred feet: a heron here, an ibis there, an alligator, or anhinga. In an environment like that, it's very hard to stay in one place. The urge to see everything is strong, but you have to make choices, so it is best to have someone scout ahead. Discuss the kinds of things you hope to find, and then let your companion walk around and take stock of what's to be seen, while you take photographs. It will relieve a lot of the pressures that draw your mind away from photography.

MOVING ON

Deciding to move from one subject to the next is a highly personal question that every photographer must solve for him or herself. However, there is a more symbolic *moving on* to deal with; a moving on to more advanced stages of the art of photography. Expanding your abilities increases the number of levels on which you can enjoy your photography. There is an excitement to each phase of the creative process: the hike, the image, the print, the exhibit, or the published work.

Take stock of your inventory, looking for technique, growth, and the need for improvement. Keep a trail diary, and compare your results with notes made in the field. One should always face new challenges, and grow in creativity and photographic involvement.

There is no greater experience for the wilderness photographer than being in working harmony with both equipment, and environment. The wilderness is there to work with, offering infinite opportunities to develop, and grow. The limits of what you can do are up to you, alone.

Index